D0522168

TO:

FROM:

WAKE UP
TO THE
JOY OF YOU

Wake Up
TO THE
Joy of You

52 MEDITATIONS AND PRACTICES
FOR A CALMER, HAPPIER, MINDFUL LIFE

AGAPI STASSINOPOULOS

BANTAM PRESS

LONDON • TORONTO • SYDNEY • AUCKLAND • JOHANNESBURG

TRANSWORLD PUBLISHERS
61–63 Uxbridge Road, London W5 5SA
www.penguin.co.uk

Transworld is part of the Penguin Random House group of companies
whose addresses can be found at global.penguinrandomhouse.com

Penguin
Random House
UK

First published in Great Britain in 2016 by Bantam Press,
an imprint of Transworld Publishers

This edition published by arrangement with Harmony Books,
an imprint of the Crown Publishing Group, a division of Penguin Random House LLC

A CIP catalogue record for this book
is available from the British Library.

ISBN 9780593078617

Typeset in 11/13.5pt Brandon Grotesque
Printed and bound by Clays Ltd, Bungay, Suffolk.

Penguin Random House is committed to a sustainable
future for our business, our readers and our planet. This book
is made from Forest Stewardship Council® certified paper.

MIX
Paper from
responsible sources
FSC® C018179

1 3 5 7 9 10 8 6 4 2

WITH IMMENSE GRATITUDE
FOR MY BELOVED TEACHER JOHN-ROGER,
WHO SHOWED ME THAT LIVING IN A STATE OF LOVING
IS THE GATEWAY TO GRACE

CONTENTS

FIND OUT WHERE JOY RESIDES,
AND GIVE IT A VOICE FAR BEYOND SINGING.
FOR TO MISS THE JOY IS TO MISS ALL.

—Robert Louis Stevenson

INTRODUCTION

"You are so real" is my favorite compliment to receive. It thrills my heart because I had to work so hard and dig through so many layers to get to my true self. It takes a lifetime to become you, and it takes a lot of trust and unlearning to be happy being you. Unraveling the mystery of who you are and how to make life work is a sacred journey. Since we only have this precious life, it's so worth doing what it takes to get to know yourself. In this book I share with you what I learned on my journey in order to help you along yours, wherever you are now. It's a road map to yourself.

Ironically, it was studying acting—the art of being other people—that led me to myself. As a student at the Royal Academy of Dramatic Art, I thought I was headed toward a glorious acting career, but I couldn't land the parts I wanted. It filled me with self-doubt, fear, insecurity. After a lot of disappointment, it dawned on me that in this life, I'm assigned to play the part of Agapi. I'm supposed to play that part fully and wholeheartedly.

We are each assigned a unique part in this magnificent universal play. Not only that, we are each supposed to write the script, direct the scenes, and produce the play. You figure it out as you go. And here's the magical thing I discovered: you have invisible cowriters, codirectors, and coproducers who will help if you let them.

But here's the catch. You have to invite them in to help write your script. You have to listen to them and trust that they will do their part. Once I learned to allow help in, I moved from feelings of loneliness and separation to a place of knowing my oneness with spirit and, through that, how I am connected to others and to my core self. Once I gave myself permission to be the unique person that I am, I began to live with a feeling of love and abundance and safety. Life became more fun and prosperous.

In my book *Unbinding the Heart*, I wrote a lot about how the events of my life shaped me and how I learned to embrace myself. But it wasn't until I took the message out to people all over the world that it dawned on me how everyone, every single person, is looking for the same thing: a connection to themselves and to each other. We all face the same challenges in this journey, they just have different packaging. Everyone is looking for the path to themselves.

You know how in fairy tales there are those helpful animals who assist you on your way home? That's what this book will be for you. It signals what you should pay attention to. It lights up the doors you may have missed and shows you where you've been keeping the keys. It leads you back to the joy of you.

This book is fifty-two light posts guiding you on the way back to yourself—one for every week of the year, although you can work at your own pace and choose which topics most speak to you. The chapters are organized to begin with the building blocks of self-care (meditation, health, making time for yourself) and with the common roadblocks to self-care (pouring your energy into other people, for example, or living in denial) and then move on to common "conflict" areas, such as relationships, money, self-esteem, anxiety, jealousy, and getting over your childhood. As you start to let go of your aches and pains, you can move to the chapters about making peace and supporting yourself. You'll learn to trust your creativity, let go of anything that no longer serves you, make your ego an ally, and keep your heart open. And finally, there are chapters about broadening your perspective and connecting to the bigger spirit that lives inside you.

Each chapter offers wisdom from a lifetime of spiritual seeking, inspiring stories, and either action plans or guided meditations to support you in letting go of what doesn't work and finding what does. Keep this book by your bedside. It is your loving companion. Be creative and have fun with it. Use it as a tool to unlock your joy and goodness. Imagine each chapter as a musical scale to practice on your way to becoming the real you. Eventually you will write your own symphony and sing your own song—the song that is waiting to be sung by you. I highly recommend you keep a journal to record your daily changes, thoughts, and shifts. It can be so self-supportive and grounding to write things down. I wrote this book with a prayer and with the intention in my heart to share all the truths I have learned along the way, and the big truth that every day, moment by moment, all you have to do is be yourself. And that's enough. Nothing more, nothing less. As we meet ourselves in all our facets, our spirit will match us and help us along the way. The miracle of your life will unfold when you stand steady on the foundation of you. Don't postpone loving yourself. Join me in this adventure to wake up to the joy of you!

1.

THE ART OF MEDITATION

"Know the world in yourself. Never look for yourself in the world."

—Ancient Egyptian proverb

From the moment you wake up to the second you fall asleep, I'm willing to bet that you are completely consumed by the outside world. There's work, relationships, finances, making dinner, getting the kids to do their homework. Your mind is filled with chatter about your kid's report card, your friend who filed for divorce, your rent, those ten pounds you need to lose . . . it's never-ending.

Reality can be the ultimate taskmaster. It will never give you a break unless you take one and create a new habit of freeing yourself from the cycle of *doing*. Most of us are so caught up in just keeping pace that we neglect our inner worlds. But there is a reason why we are called human beings and not human doings.

Your inner world has nothing to do with your thoughts, your emotions, your unpaid bills, or your worries about whether your partner really loves you. In order to move past these worldly concerns that can consume you, I like to imagine being in a plane. As you ascend, the city below looks otherworldly, with small patches of green and minute toy houses. You feel a sense of detachment, elevation, and perspective. The noise of the world quiets.

This is one of the reasons why I love to fly: I can think clearly, find solutions to challenging situations, and feel gratitude for the mystery of being alive. I always promise myself that when I land safely, I'll never worry again. Then I land and pick up my worries at the baggage claim. That's why I meditate. To bring back that feeling of a higher perspective.

Meditation involves going deeper into who you are. D. H. Lawrence wrote, "Let us lose sight of ourselves, and break the mirrors. For the fierce curve of our lives is moving again to the depths out of sight, in the deep living heart." There is this yearning in all of us to go deeper, to get to your heart, to your being. To know yourself beyond your identity. Any form of meditation in which you disconnect from the outside world can be one of the most supportive and effective things you can do to shift daily stresses and find your way to your own being. And little by little you'll learn to undo the tension that has accumulated in your body so you can begin to relax and let go.

People often tell me that they've tried meditation but given up because they couldn't escape looping thoughts and worries. They tell me meditating makes them more anxious than they were already. I understand. In fact, I've been there! Finding the sweet spot of peace and balance so you're simply present, beyond all the chatter, takes practice. Don't be discouraged, just keep going. I love this quote from Steve Jobs, a lifelong practitioner of meditation: "If you just sit and observe, you will see how restless your mind is. If you try to calm it, it only makes it worse, but over time it does calm, and when it does, there's room to hear subtler things—that's when your intuition starts to blossom and you start to see things more clearly and be in the present more. Your mind just slows down, and you see a tremendous expanse in the moment. You see so much more than you could see before."

The practice of meditation is ancient. It's been a part of daily life in Eastern civilizations for centuries. In the West, stress and burnout has led us to look toward the East and learn from that tradition. Meditation, along with yoga, has gone mainstream—a great addition to our culture. The most essential ingredient for these practices is heartfelt devotion. If you are meditating without devotion, the results won't be as rich as they could be. It can't just be another thing to check off your to-do list.

There's a beautiful prayer by a Benedictine nun: "Dear God, show me the truth about myself no matter how beautiful it is." If you are struggling with meditation, I suggest starting your daily practice with a heartfelt prayer, which can take the form of a poem that moves you or a lovely picture of a sunset, a garden, a mountaintop, the ocean—whatever moves you, calms you, and connects you with the wonders of life. Picture someone you love in your heart, and bring your whole self and your senses into it.

In that moment of true connection, you'll find there are no distractions. You are present in your heart. Do it in the way that's wonderfully particular to you, just make sure you put your heart in it. Don't ever worry about emptying your mind, because that's not going to happen. What you're doing is refocusing your mind to whatever lifts you.

So often, people share with me that when they sit quietly with nothing to do, focusing on their breath or a word, they start to see their faults and inadequacies. They find it's dark inside. Recognize that this "nothingness" is really *no-thing*—that it's the absence of thoughts, personality, and the material world. Sit with it. You'll find that behind the emptiness is something bigger—the richness of your spirit.

Here are my meditation tips. If you start to feel upset about something, don't fight it, don't judge it, just observe it, relax, and breathe into it. There's a good chance the disturbance will diminish or evaporate if you don't keep feeding it.

Meditating is similar to strengthening muscles at the gym. Like exercising, it takes practice, persistence, and commitment. You never know when it will click. At some point, you'll be sitting down, chanting and observing your breath, and wow, something opens up and you are aware that you have entered a lovely, quiet, still place inside yourself.

I find that meditation is all about connecting to a loving, accepting, and centered part of myself, which I call my "calm." You don't have to be sitting under a mango tree to get the experience. It can happen anywhere. Don't limit yourself, you can meditate in the car, in the bathtub, in your office, at a restaurant, on the train to work, definitely on a plane. It's great if you have a sacred place in your home where you can build this energy, but sometimes people will stop meditating because they think it has to be at a particular time and place. No! You can take a few minutes anywhere you are. For my mother, washing dishes or cooking for friends and family was her prayer, her meditation, her ritual of reverence. "All of us eating together is my human communion," she'd say. She meditated in her own distinctive way—feeding seagulls at the beach, dancing outside on a rainy day.

If we don't involve our heartfelt spirit in everything we do—including meditation—we deny ourselves a rich life. Imagine if you lived every moment connected with your inner self, your invisible soul. If you knew for sure that meditating could connect you to your soul, wouldn't you want to start practicing and keep going no matter what? Meditation, yoga, or any spiritual practice can become a joyful journey to your soul.

It's wondrous how much creativity and insight can open for us as we become receptive and listen to our spirit, which can always guide us through our inner and outer life. Often after meditating, solutions appear; inspiration shows up. I write poetry, run into someone I've been wanting to connect with—there's plenty of time to do everything I want, things miraculously fall into place.

Meditation is an incredibly powerful tool. A regular practice can result in a more fulfilling life. You'll start to drop your agenda of what your life should be like and open up to your higher purpose. By meditating with devotion, it's possible to become so in tune with yourself that you'll never have to read another book about being happy. You'll be living your own testament of happiness. It's possible to live joyfully, feeling connected to your own source. Life is a combination lock and you have the code to open it. With practice and devotion, you will unlock the door to reveal a more magnificent and resilient you.

GUIDED MEDITATION

Close your eyes and get into a comfortable position. Take a deep breath and as you exhale, breathe out any tension, anxiety, and worry. And as you inhale, start to breathe in a sense of peace, beauty, relaxation, and sweetness. Focus on your heart and with every breath allow your heart to expand, to fill you with a heartfelt energy. Imagine that your whole body is enveloped in this heartfelt energy, then lift yourself higher into the top of your head. Imagine that you are much larger than your body. Start imagining a beautiful light all around you until you experience being fully enveloped by that light. Focus your intention behind your eyes as if you are sitting in a comfortable space behind your eyes. As you go beyond your personality, emotions, and thoughts, reflect for a moment on these questions: Who am I? Am I my body? Am I my thoughts? Am I my feelings or circumstances? Am I my name, my friends, my ambition, my bank account? Am I my feelings of less or more, or am I part of something so much larger, connected to the source? And then, start to see something bigger, more beautiful than you have ever imagined.

Lift the curtain and the veil so you can begin to see *you* beyond your image of what you look like in this world, into the essence of your radiance. Allow yourself to be quiet, to be still, knowing you can trust your life force, your soul, your spirit to show you more of who you are. And just observe to see what is revealed to you. Listen to guidance for inspiration and for grace. Breathe it in, allow it in the depths of your heart and receive it. Nothing to do, nowhere to go, just calm. Stay there for a few minutes. As long as you want. Build this calmness until it becomes your foundation. Return to that place throughout the day, as many times as you can. Now, whenever you're ready, fill your lungs and whole body with oxygen, gently exhale, open your eyes, shake your shoulders, wriggle your fingers and toes, and when you stand up, open your arms and exhale with a long sigh, "Ahh." One more time, "Ahh." Give yourself a big hug.

2.

ARE YOU A PEOPLE FIXER?

Everybody talks about wanting to change things and help and fix, but ultimately all you can do is fix yourself. And that's a lot. Because if you can fix yourself, it has a ripple effect.

—Rob Reiner

I often struggle with wanting people to be happy and feel a sense of responsibility if they are not. Especially the people I love and care for. When I see them disturbed, upset, or struggling, my whole heart tries to help them find a state of happiness. It's such a twisted feeling, hoping to fix someone whose patterns, emotions, and feelings happen independent of you. This desire to help is rooted in me from childhood, when I tried to lift my father's heavy heart and make him happy.

It wasn't just about my dad. This desire transferred to my relationships with men and to my friendships. I attracted people who would come to me with their problems, and I'd become consumed with trying to help them. For years, my identity was wrapped up in making other people happy. I had no boundaries. If I entered a room and sensed someone was unhappy, I assigned myself the role of getting them out of their unhappiness and lifting them up, which can be exhausting and not a lot of fun.

My personal power, confidence, and self-esteem were in direct proportion to how much I helped others. You might be the same way. Operating this way in life can actually suck out a lot of your own personal energy and make you feel depleted, as if you have a leaky faucet that your energy is escaping from. Becoming aware that the faucet is leaking is the beginning of action. Then, recognize you have to back off and allow people their own experience and process. Your responsibility is to bring your own energy back to you.

If you love helping others, you might want to consider becoming a counselor. But if that's not what you want, ask yourself some fundamental questions about what drives you to feel worthy of your own happiness. Do you believe that you are only allowed to be happy if other people are happy? That type of altruism has its roots in feeling unworthy. The belief is "I don't have a right to my own joy and happiness unless other people around me are happy." I've often thought about the origin of that belief; it could very well be a way to avoid looking at your own life, your own pain, your own desires, and your own dreams.

When I was younger, I had a lot of things I wanted to achieve, but I didn't know how. I felt very insecure, and my confidence was shaken when my career as an actress wasn't happening. Taking care of people became a source of solace, it gave me a sense of purpose and satisfaction. It's very important to be ruthless with yourself and say, "Is this pattern serving or sabotaging me?"

Each one of us has been dealt a set of cards. None of us is given a complete deck. But we are all given a trump card, the truth that something bigger than ourselves is working through us. This applies to everyone. My saving grace is that when I see people who are going through a tough time, I remember that something bigger in me is also in them. I ask myself to forgo any sense of responsibility and not to presume to know what's going on with them. I'm not their savior. You can have distance as well as compassion, and you can know that there is a solution for them and they will get through to the other side. That they will grow and evolve and learn what they've come here to learn. You can support other people without trying to fix them. You can share wisdom, point the way, offer another perspective, be a sounding board or a safe haven. Offer practical solutions and help them see options. These are very powerful ways that I have allowed other people to be there for me and that I've been there for other people. That's the gift we all have to comfort, to lift, and to inspire others.

So, if you are a people fixer, I challenge you to question why you are doing that: What is the benefit and what is the reward? What is the tape running in your head stating that you don't have a right to your happiness unless other people are happy? You can erase the old beliefs and realize that there is tremendous grace in allowing people their own experiences and processes.

Remember the powerful Serenity Prayer: "God grant me the serenity to accept the things I cannot change; courage to change the things I can; and wisdom to know the difference." Be aware of where you place your energy, your thoughts, and your emotions. Your first responsibility is to yourself. That's the greatest gift we can give to each other.

GUIDED MEDITATION

Sit comfortably in a relaxed position; close your eyes and take a deep breath and exhale. As you exhale, breathe out any feelings of tension, preoccupations, burdens, and worries. Just come to the present, right here, right now. As you take your next breath, receive your breath and observe the rising and the falling of your breath until you become more relaxed, calm, and centered. Visualize a beautiful, calm wave entering your heart, your mind, and your emotions. As you exhale, breathe out any turbulence, any feelings that you should be or do anything other than what you're doing or being. This is a moment for you. Focus on your belly, the center of where the emotions reside, where your power base is, your willpower—your solar plexus—and start to breathe deeply into that center. Place your right hand on your heart and your left hand on your belly. Imagine that there is a bridge connecting them. Make this bridge filled with sturdiness, strength, and stability. See yourself crossing this bridge and connecting your two centers: your heart and your power center.

Imagine cords and energies that attach to other people in your life. Family, friends, people you know, people you love and care about that have part of your energy extended to them. Start to cut those cords. Literally take your hands and start to cut these cords between you and other people. As you take your next breath, take in all this energy that has been going out—to trying to fix things, fix people, make things better—and draw it back to you. With every breath imagine that this energy is coming back to you, is filling you, and making you calm, strong, and protected. Start to feel a sense of wholeness, completeness, and peace. Really scan your own consciousness to see if there are any hidden energies going out to people you care about, people you want to see acting or being different, and without any hesitation, pull the energies back, cut the cords between you

and them, and see them in perfect health and well-being.
Keep sending energy to your heart, then back to your center, and filling yourself with love, calmness, and a sense of
completion.

Know that all is in perfect balance and that we have all
the resources we need to make our lives work. Place your
hands back on your heart and imagine that an energy of
light and radiance is filling you and extending to all those
in your consciousness, all the situations and all the circumstances, from all your light and inner radiance. Start to send
it out with a sense of compassion. Affirm that there is nothing for you to do but keep an open heart filled with grace.
*All shall be well, and all shall be well, and all manner of thing
shall be well.*

3.

MAKE YOUR HEALTH A PRIORITY

You have to learn how to listen to your body, going with it and not against it, avoiding all effort or strain . . . You will be amazed to discover that, if you are kind to your body, it will respond in an incredible way.

—Vanda Scaravelli

Consider this:

→ We have 37.2 trillion cells in our bodies (compare that to the 400 billion stars in the galaxy!).

→ The cells that make up your body are dying and then being replaced all the time. By the time you've read this sentence, roughly 25 million cells will have died, but you'll make 300 billion more as your day unfolds.

→ Your brain is 2 percent of your body's weight but uses 20 percent of its oxygen intake.

→ Your brain generates twelve to twenty-five watts of electricity.

- Your brain is 73 percent water, and just 2 percent dehydration affects attention, memory, and other cognitive skills. (Therefore, hydrate, hydrate, hydrate!)

- The average brain has about fifty thousand thoughts per day . . . and 70 percent are believed to be negative.

- The brain's storage capacity is virtually unlimited.

- Ninety-five percent of your decision making takes place in your subconscious mind.

- The brain in your head isn't your only brain. There's a second brain in your intestines that contains 100,000 neurons. Gut bacteria are responsible for producing over thirty neurotransmitters, including the "happy" molecule serotonin.

- The human eye can see the difference between around 10 million shades of color.

- Eyes never sleep. The human eye is the only part of our bodies that can function at 100 percent of its abilities day or night, whenever we need it. Your eyes don't actually get tired!

- We have 640 muscles, 206 bones, thirty-two teeth, and four vocal cords (two true and two false cords).

Take a moment in reverence of the miracle of life you are.

We have nothing to do with making this miracle happen; it's working in spite of us, our inexhaustible life force. Yet we take all this for granted. We worry that our breasts are too small, our butt too big, or our nose too long. If you ever feel insecure, insignificant, or inadequate, remember that there are more cells in your body than stars in the galaxy.

There were many times when I took my health for granted, which is normal to do until something goes wrong. If I felt tired, I never thought to look at exercise, diet, or vitamins to increase my level of energy. However, when my body started to change with menopause, it struck me that I needed to pay more attention to it and make a greater investment in my well-being. I felt a huge responsibility to care for my body. My body was changing, and I started to gain weight that I couldn't seem to lose. It took me by surprise. Having hot flashes and sweats, and feeling like I didn't have control of my own body, I dove into research: reading books, asking others for advice, trying different kinds of foods, and finding forms of exercise that energized me.

But the key factor in helping me get a handle on this physical change was finding the right doctor to advise me about what hormones my body needed to feel balanced. It was trial and error—at first, just error. Unfortunately, the first doctor I saw, despite his prestigious reputation, gave me so much estrogen that my breasts grew two sizes. I felt off! After this, I started asking other women whom they would recommend. I'm thankful that I found a great doctor who gave me the right dose of natural estrogen and progesterone and kept in touch for weekly monitoring. We continue to adjust my dosages as needed, and now my body feels more balanced and happy. Since making my health a priority, I aim to find doctors I can develop a personal relationship with, where I feel like more than just a "patient." I'm not saying that hormone treatment is right for you, but do prioritize finding doctors who treat you holistically, who really pay attention to you.

We all desire energy, vitality, and strength so we can be productive and creative. That requires each one of us to map out what we need to maintain our optimal vitality. Isn't it ironic how things like work commitments, relationships, school, social endeavors, or even appearance often take precedence over self-care—when self-care is the foundation of your whole life?

My sister has become an evangelist for sleep, and living with her has shifted me from a night owl to someone who seeks to be in bed by midnight. I used to be compulsive about finishing my e-mails so that I wouldn't have to face them the next day. I soon discovered that I was better off dealing with my e-mail the next day, well rested. Putting down my devices at least one hour before going to sleep helps me transition from a full day to a restful night. My sister gave me a quote that I keep by my bedside: "A good day starts the night before." As much as I love the aliveness and creativity I feel in the late hours of the evening, I realized that the price I paid the next day in feeling tired, sluggish, and anxious was too big. I found important habits to help shift from wakefulness to sleep—taking a hot bath, playing calm music, reading some poetry, lighting a candle, and not watching TV. Sleep is not just for my body but for my brain—it's when my brain downloads, uploads, sends to trash, and reboots so I awaken the next day refreshed. What's more, sleep deprivation is directly related to weight issues, diabetes, high blood pressure, and heart disease. When I improved the quality of my sleep, I lost weight. Now I know that my 37.2 trillion cells are very grateful for my new sleep habits. To dive deeper, read Arianna Huffington's book *The Sleep Revolution*. Remember that sleep is also a spiritual practice where we receive our inner direction: "In a dream, a vision of the night, when sound sleep falls on men, while they slumber in their beds, then He opens the ears of men, and seals their instruction" (Job 33:15–16).

As much as I know how great supplements are for me, I still resist taking them. So I have come up with a couple of strategies. I keep my "nonnegotiable" vitamins (probiotics, vitamin D, magnesium, and curcumin) by my bathroom sink to take after brushing my teeth. I carry the rest of my vitamins in little ziplock bags in my handbag. To encourage myself to take these pills, I have researched what each vitamin can do for my organs. I also did two genetic tests that told me what I'm prone to, what I need to be aware of, what my risk factors are, and which foods are good for me. I recommend that you learn as much as you can about your own body.

One thing is true for all of us: cane sugar negatively affects your liver, insulin levels, weight, and proneness to inflammation. I know that when I have sugar, my energy plummets after spiking, my mouth gets dry at night, and my eyes are puffy in the morning. So I watch my intake. Since I'm Greek and I'm not the kind of person who is satisfied with kale and quinoa salad, I make sure that what I eat is healthy, lean, and always filled with flavor. I learned from my mother to make eating a ritual; she abhorred "fast food"—a meal is a time for good, uplifting conversation and connection. Another good habit from my mother: carry delicious, nutritious snacks in your bag like nuts and apples with almond butter. And always drink plenty of water.

In a culture that obsesses about weight, I had to find my own balance and happiness with my size and shape. I now think more about my healthy habits and less about my weight. I'm not a vegetarian or vegan. I'm Greek. I love lamb and beef, but I aim to eat organic and grass-fed. Another drastic change I made was switching from regular milk to almond milk, and now I no longer feel bloated. I learned to always read labels before I buy anything because there are so many hidden sugars, even those that are labeled "natural." If I do eat something that isn't nutritious, I make sure that I don't eat my judgment as well. I think, "Hey, this crème brulée is not nutritious, but I love it and I'm totally going to enjoy it." That's what I call awareness without denial.

It's just as important to relieve the tension of our bodies with touch. There is a direct link between physical touch and psychological well-being: when we are touched, oxytocin, the "cuddle hormone," is released, and we feel happier and more connected. Our bodies need to be touched, nurtured, and loved. Research affordable massages in your area and take advantage as often as you can. Use essential oils and aromatherapy at home for daily nurturing—they can have a positive impact on your mood.

Honor your body, treat it with respect, and learn about it, because it is a microcosm of the cosmos. Serve it well, so it can serve you in your life. Practice compassion and fully engage in your well-being. You deserve it.

SUGGESTIONS FOR THIS WEEK

1. Identify the areas you need to address to take care of your health. Record in your journal how you're implementing microsteps to improve your health and energy level.

2. Research anything you're curious about that has to do with your body and its well-being, for example, how food affects your body, or what supplements can meet your needs. When you have an annual physical, if there's anything that

needs further diagnosis, build your tribe of doctors, from general practitioner to integrative medicine, to help you feel better.

If you want to have a genetic test, try one of the following labs: 23andme.com, Genova Diagnostic Lab (gdx.net), or greatplainslaboratory.com.

3. Remember that daily movement, hydration, nutritious food, and good sleep are the four major pillars of a healthy life.

GUIDED MEDITATION

Find a comfortable place and lie down. If you're in bed, place a pillow under your knees and behind your head and start to relax your breath. Take a deep breath and exhale with a sound, exhaling all of the tensions, "Ahh." And receive your inhalation. Start to observe the rising and falling of your breath, deepening the breath. Start to experience your whole body softening and releasing the tension. Experience how the surface below you supports you and imagine that you are lying on a cushion of vital, healthy grass. It is green. It is soft. It is luscious. Fill yourself with a vibrant, green healing light. Imagine that the sun is bathing your whole body and there is a beautiful breeze blowing across your face, wafting away any worries or anxieties or concerns of the day. Relax your jaw, relax your neck, relax your shoulders, the back of your spine, your buttocks, your thighs, your knees, your calves, your feet, your arms, your hands.

Open your palms toward the sun and feel the energy

and heat of the sun in your hands. Breathe in the warmth of this golden light and pour it from the top of your head to your spine, to your bones, to your chest, expanding your rib cage, relaxing your diaphragm, and filling all the organs of your body with light: heart, liver, spleen, pancreas, kidneys, stomach, intestines, colon, sexual organs, your blood, veins, muscles, bones, all the way down to your toes. Let this light travel to your fingers, nails, elbows, arms, and all the way back up your spine. Feel your face muscles relaxing and visualize this light flowing into your eye sockets and see the light moving inside your head infusing your brain with a golden light. This light is moving inside your head all the way down your spine and connects your head with your tailbone. It is making everything healthy, vital, alive, filled with good energy and vitality.

Allow yourself to soak in all this good energy, relax knowing that this body of yours is a miracle of life, performing at its best. Send the depths of your gratitude to your 37.2 trillion cells and say, "I love you, I appreciate you, and I will take care of you better and better every day." Ask the intelligence of your body, "What can I give you to make you healthier, more productive, vital, and full of energy and make you feel more loved?" Listen to the wisdom of your body as it answers. Is it something that your body needs more of, or less of, on any level—physical, emotional, mental, or spiritual? As you listen, make a mental note and see yourself doing what your body is asking. Send a message of love to every part of your body, a message of reverence and gratitude. Revel in the miracle of life that you are.

Smile inside and out, and as you gently open your eyes, stretch your arms high with a deep breath and exhale with a sound, "Ahh." Take another deep breath and exhale with a sound, "Ahh." This time as you breathe in, fill your lungs with air and take both your arms and give yourself a big hug—literally holding yourself so dear. Stretch your arms, neck, and feet. Expand your field of energy to encompass this beautiful bright light. Gently role your neck to the right and left, and whenever you're ready, slowly come back, feeling your aliveness, grounded and filled with vitality, energy, and radiance.

4.

THE ART OF DOING NOTHING

You must have a room, or a certain hour or so a day, where you don't know what was in the newspapers that morning, you don't know who your friends are, you don't know what you owe anybody, you don't know what anybody owes to you. This is a place where you can simply experience and bring forth what you are and what you might be. This is the place of creative incubation. At first you may find that nothing happens there. But if you have a sacred place and use it, something eventually will happen.

—Joseph Campbell, *The Power of Myth*

This is one of my favorite quotes of all time. When I find a quiet place at home and still myself, forgetting my own preoccupations and tapping into something deeper than my own identity, it's incredibly freeing. If you spend five to ten minutes a day in that state of forgetting who you think you are, you will tap into who you truly are, and in this state you can experience pure bliss.

The journalist Eric Barker expressed the same message in terms that are more relevant in today's world: "Those who can sit in a chair, undistracted for hours, mastering subjects and creating things will rule the world—while the rest of us frantically and futilely try to keep up the texts, tweets, and other incessant interruptions."

Let's follow this great advice right now, before you delve into this chapter. Take a deep breath and exhale. Relax. Now, do nothing. And I mean nothing. Nothing in your head, nothing to say. Suspend all your worries, your future pursuits, concerns about other people, as though you're putting up a big white canvas in front of you, with nothing on it. Take time to pause and do nothing.

Do you know that one of the best ways to be creative and productive is to give yourself a break? As Michel de Montaigne said, "They have only stepped back in order to leap farther." It's similar to how there are white spaces, gaps, in art. Pausing is a part of music. In every symphony, there are rests between the notes—this pause is honored and treated with great reverence. Harold Pinter, the well-known English playwright, wrote pauses into his plays, in between the lines, indicating how long each actor should wait before delivering the next line. When I was studying theater, I learned how important these pauses were for dramatic effect; they were never empty, but instead filled with silence and were called "pregnant pauses."

When I ask people, "When was the last time you did nothing?" they can't remember and confess they're fearful of being left behind. When we have to wait at an airport or a doctor's office, we always fill the minutes with texting, e-mailing, reading, talking, being frustrated, making a mental to-do list of everything that needs to get done. But consider this: you could reflect on things that matter to you. You *could* just do nothing and give yourself time to wonder.

We are all addicted to technology. Social media demands so much of us, and we are consumed by being connected. This fills up the spaces where otherwise our creativity could flourish, where we could wonder. You have the ability to stop, let your mind wander, allow new creative thoughts and ideas to come to you, tune into your own breath, embrace your own being in a moment of quiet. This is sacred. You can refine the art of doing nothing when you're alone at home—in the bathtub, swinging in a hammock, sitting in a rocking chair on the front porch—or strolling through the park, walking along the beach, feeding the seagulls, just being with yourself. That's when your intuitive inner self can emerge.

One of my favorite things to do as a little girl was to swing aimlessly. It gave me such joy and took away the pressure that I was feeling; it was my time to really wonder. As Veronique Vienne wrote in her book *The Art of Doing Nothing*, "For a child doing nothing doesn't mean being inactive. It means doing something that doesn't have a name." I remember a time when I went fishing with a fisherman in the Greek islands at dawn. It was enthralling to watch him so patiently waiting to catch the fish, watching the line to see if it moved. Witnessing his stillness in the calmness of the sea, I felt completely present and at peace.

Doing nothing isn't just about feeling good. Vienne also wrote, "Some of the best thinking we do happens when the conscious mind is on sabbatical. Isaac Newton figured out the law of universal gravitation when sitting under a tree. Ben Franklin invented the lightning rod while flying a kite. Thomas Edison came up with the light-bulb filament while idly rolling kerosene residue between his fingers. Albert Einstein pondered the riddle of the universe with a cat on his lap." What an endorsement for doing nothing! Who knows what you might discover and contribute to society!

Doing nothing is not meditation—that can become one more thing to do. I'm talking about free-falling with yourself. Staring, gazing. Did you know that gazing is a spiritual practice—you can gaze at the horizon until you expand your vision into something larger than yourself, and merge with this expansiveness. Doing nothing can open you up to the awe of your life, the mystery of who you are. It's remarkable what happens when you slow down. No longer operating from "time famine," you'll feel timeless.

There are a lot of Eastern practices that involve this non-doing, this non-effort, this leaning back and surrendering. However, in the West, we train our minds in such a linear way, constantly pushing ourselves to produce. We feel guilty when we're not producing. We are programmed to do, not to be. We tell ourselves that if we're not accomplishing, we will fall behind. So we often feel pressured and anxious and keep moving to relieve that anxiety. But, as Rumi said, "You wander from room to room, hunting for the diamond necklace that's already around your neck."

Return to that calm place inside of you often. Build it until it becomes your way of being. Imagine how amazing life would be if you did things from that place of no effort. I encourage you to give yourself this gift of finding creative ways to do nothing.

SUGGESTIONS FOR THIS WEEK

1. Make it a habit to watch the sun set and appreciate the slow-motion transition from day to night. Take the colors in and notice how each sunset varies from day to day. Gaze upon the horizon and allow your eyes to soften. Fill your heart with gratitude and awe.

2. Throughout each day, make it a habit to pause and get back to your own natural breath and internal rhythm. Back away from your to-do list. Take a walk around your space, leaving your

phones behind, wherever you are; just five to ten minutes of slowing down will energize you.

3. Find a place in your home where you can "lean back," allowing yourself to let go of "the next thing" and all the things that are preoccupying you. Stare, be, and breathe—there is no urgency.

5

HOW TO HANDLE NEGATIVE PEOPLE

If you can cultivate the right attitude, your enemies are your best spiritual teachers because their presence provides you with the opportunity to enhance and develop tolerance, patience and understanding.

—The Dalai Lama

One afternoon, a close friend of mine and her six-year-old daughter came to visit me after seeing my friend's sister, who was going through a bitter divorce. When they came in, I gave them big hugs and asked, "How was everything with Aunt Mary?" The little girl said, in a matter-of-fact way, "Aunt Mary is very negative, Agapi, because she's unhappy." There you have it, from the mouths of babes. Why are negative people negative? They are unhappy! Now, that doesn't justify their behavior, nor does it suggest that you have a responsibility to fix these people and their issues. Your main responsibility is to yourself and it's up to you how you react to negative people. Have compassion and leave them alone.

We have all known and encountered negative people through-out our lives. We can stumble across them in the cashier line, at the airport, at the bank, on the bus . . . negative people are everywhere! An interaction can be fleeting but still affect you. And it's an even bigger challenge when the negative person is in your close personal circle. It could be your significant other, best friend, mother-in-law, boss, your child's teacher. No matter whether it's personal or impersonal, these interactions can have an impact on your life.

Don't you wish there was an 800 number where you could report negative people and they could be fined for their attitude? After a certain number of complaints, they wouldn't be allowed to interact with other people until they changed their behavior. Since we don't have this kind of accountability system, let me share with you what I've learned.

My father had a tendency to be negative, especially when things hadn't gone his way or when he had lost money at the horse races. It could also happen at a restaurant; if the food wasn't served in a timely fashion, he would explode at the waiter. When you're twelve years old, it's very hard to yell back and say, "Dad, stop behaving like that and be nice to people," so I had to find another way to cope. In order to protect myself from his behavior, I would shut down and withdraw. I developed a habit of censoring myself to deescalate the situation, and this stayed with me throughout my life. Often when people acted negatively, I would go into denial, making excuses, saying that they were just having a bad day. But then I realized that some people were like the character Ouiser, played by Shirley MacLaine in *Steel Magnolias*, who says, "I've just been in a very bad mood for forty years." Some people wake up and go to sleep in a negative frame of mind.

As I became aware of my pattern, I started to find different ways to handle negativity. The most important thing that I learned for dealing with negative people is to stop taking it personally.

Even if these people are close to me, their behavior has nothing to do with me. I realized that I had a choice of whether to tolerate or react to the situation.

There are lots of ways to react to negativity. You are absolutely allowed to tell someone, in a centered and calm way, "You know, you're expressing yourself in negative way right now." Make sure you don't call the person "negative," because there's judgment in that; only talk about the way they are expressing themselves in the moment. And say, "There's another way to express yourself. You have a choice to shift your attitude if you're interested in exploring it, and I think if you tried, you might be happier." You have a right to tell someone how they are affecting you and give them feedback; if they hear it enough, it might sink in that things need to change.

Another way to handle a situation like that is to tell yourself, "I've just encountered a negative person" and not react, but experiment with sending positive energy their way. And then just get out of the way. If you are waiting in line, go to another line; if you're talking to a customer service representative, hang up and call again. The same rule applies when this negativity is with the people in your home or in your closest circle. You always have a choice to move away. You should never feel like you have to put up with it, endure, and then end up feeling victimized and resentful. I know that these people may be your mother, child, or landlord, but my advice is to create a strategy that keeps you in your own center, and that may mean announcing that you're taking a "time-out" physically and mentally to help yourself regroup. This may take a few minutes, hours, or days—whatever you need to stay in that centered place. No matter where you go, what you do, always hold your positive energy, so you're never trapped in another person's cycle of negativity.

A friend of mine married a woman who started nagging and became very negative toward him; he could never do anything right. One day, while she was out, he moved his belongings out of their home and left a note saying, "You have thirty-two days to work on your behavior. Contact me after and let me know if you want to have a loving relationship. Otherwise, we will be filing for a divorce." She was stunned and threw a fit, but then it hit home, and she started to make adjustments.

Another friend dealt with toxic people at work. She tried every technique imaginable. She sent positive energy and tried to stay in her own positive headspace, but no matter what, two of her colleagues were still extremely negative toward her. She went to her boss and asked for mediation, but he wouldn't entertain the idea and even threatened to fire her. She stayed for another six months before deciding she had to move on and get another job. After she left, she said to me, "My life is too precious to spend it deflecting negative people." She found an amazing job where everyone was respectful and appreciative of her work.

If your life is full of these petty tyrants, ask yourself, "Why am I attracting these challenging people in my life and what are they here to teach me?" The answer could be that they're in your life to strengthen you, so that you learn to stand up for yourself. It could be that they're there to show you that you're strong enough not to be impacted by them. Find out which lesson you need to learn.

Maybe the lesson is that you're in a negative place yourself. When I'm in a bad mood, I attract negative people. Attracting negativity can be a reflection of what you're putting out there— check it out! If I want to attract other kinds of people, I first need to shift my negative attitude.

Maybe on some level, you feel you deserve bad treatment,

and that's why you keep allowing it into your life. This is something you really have to ask yourself: "Why do I think I deserve this?" It might not look like abuse because you don't have any bruises and no one is screaming curse words at you, but psychically it's still abuse if someone in your life is consistently negative toward you, and you must take steps to protect yourself. A friend of mine has a very negative mother who never stops criticizing, nagging, and complaining. My friend gets totally depleted around her, so we worked on a practice called "Portable Paradise." You solidify your inner environment so that outer circumstances don't pull you down. She said to me, "I can hold my center and inner calm for about an hour with my mother." So she set a strict boundary with her mother, only allowing her to visit for one hour at time. It wasn't easy, but it's what she needed. You'll learn to create your own Portable Paradise in this chapter's meditation.

The greatest mistake you can make is to try to fix people. Say you have a fabulous idea and when you share it at the dinner table, your husband says, "That's a stupid idea." Or maybe he totally ignores you, which is another way of being negative. As a result, you start to feel deflated. In personal relationships, it's very important to call people on what they're doing and to stop tolerating it. Be honest, give feedback to people. Always taking care of yourself is your primary responsibility. Fill yourself with so much light and goodness that you rise to your spirit of positivity. Your light will shine so bright that it lightens the darkness.

SUGGESTIONS FOR THIS WEEK

1. Take an inventory of your life and look at the areas where you get caught up in a negative cycle. Is it a thought, a situation, or a person? Ask yourself, "Where do I need to detach,

observe, and disconnect from what's affecting me and make wiser choices?" Write these down in your journal to ground your awareness; bring your light into it.

2. Be ruthless with yourself in insisting that if you are around negative energy, you will remove yourself from the situation and not let it affect you. Know your bandwidth and stick to it.

3. Build your Portable Paradise and do the following meditation to solidify your inner environment of peace and calm that no one will disturb.

GUIDED MEDITATION

Find a comfortable location where you won't be interrupted. Take a deep breath and exhale any tensions, any worries, any preoccupations from the day. Allow yourself to relax, and come deeper into your own breath, breathing in, slowing down the breath and exhaling. Breathing in on a count of 4 . . . 1 . . . 2 . . . 3 . . . 4, exhaling . . . 4 . . . 3 . . . 2 . . . 1. Filling your heart and lungs with your breath. Observe the rising and falling of your breath. Bring into your awareness a place that you've been in your life where you like to go, where you feel calm, relaxed, centered, and serene. Bring it to your awareness as vividly as possible. Is it indoors, outdoors? How does the air feel? Is there a breeze? Is it sunny? Is it fragrant? What are the sounds you hear? Bring yourself there, right now. Allow yourself to bring all of you present—your mind, your emotions, and your whole being—as if you are there right now. Imagine a color that you love—it's permeating the air of this place. Imagine that this color is as exquisite, as vibrant and vivid as possible. If it's green, make it the best green you have ever seen. If it's blue, imagine it brighter than you have ever seen. Take this color that you love through your whole body.

As you exhale this time, see yourself standing, walking, going through this beautiful place that you love and ever so grounded in it, notice the things that are around this place, the sounds that you hear, and in your head, say a word you love that brings you peace. It could be a word like *beautiful*, *joyful*, *rested*, *calm*, *centered*, *abundant*, *vibrant*, *positive*, or *warm*. It could be a name or anything that makes you feel really connected. Let this word vibrate through your whole being and consciousness. When you are ready, take your right hand and put it over your heart and anchor this feeling. Take your left hand and put it on your belly. Anchor this feeling in your solar plexus, and feel safe and at home with yourself. When you are ready, take a deep breath and let this place be really anchored in your body, knowing you can return here any time during your day. This is your Portable Paradise—you can take it anywhere you want to go. Take a deep breath and exhale with a sound, "Ahh." When you are ready, wriggle your toes and hands. Shake your shoulders. Stretch your neck left and right, and gently open your eyes and be back here, and open your hands, your arms, and make a big circle all around you with a sound that's like "Ahh." Take another deep breath and make a sound, and give thanks for the knowledge that you have this place inside of you. It's your Portable Paradise and it's with you whenever you need it.

6.

THERE IS NOTHING WRONG WITH YOU

When my parents decided to separate, I was twelve. My father, a concentration camp survivor, suffered from melancholia. I so wanted my father to be happy and longed for my parents to love one another. I wished I could fix it all. I couldn't, of course, and the question loomed, "What's wrong with me that I can't fix my father and make my parents happy?"

What's wrong with me? It's what I asked when I was a child who didn't understand that my parents' marriage was far beyond my control. It's what so many of us ask ourselves when relationships fail, when we can't get pregnant, when we can't find work that fulfills us, when we get fired, when we struggle with addiction.

Hear me loud and clear: There is nothing wrong with you.

A friend of mine tried to get his BA but failed a crucial exam twice. He kept asking, "What's wrong with me that keeps me from passing this test?" He could have asked that question forever with no answer. Instead, he realized he didn't care about getting a degree; what he really wanted was to develop his own business. When he directed his energy toward his business idea, he excelled. Turns out it was his parents who cared about the degree, not him.

I've had similar experiences. When I was pursuing my acting career and didn't get parts I'd auditioned for, I'd ask myself, "What's wrong with me?" Then one day, I stopped trying to figure out what was wrong with me and realized, "This is no longer working for me." It was a huge relief. I dropped the burden of blame. I banished the feelings of inadequacy. I moved into self-acceptance and saw the opportunities available to me in other fields. I remember trying to produce a big television series about the gods of Greece, but when all the parts weren't coming together, I had to reflect and really figure out what I wanted to do. The answer was that I wanted to express my talent and my creativity to contribute to the uplifting of others. So I decided to produce my own one-woman show with my favorite stories of the goddesses. This became a great success.

When things don't work out and you find yourself thinking, "What's wrong with me?," here's what you do: flip that thought into "This was not meant for me," and find what is yours to do. We get into trouble when we pursue what is not meant for us.

If you believe that there is something wrong with you, you'll mistake an outside obstacle for an inner flaw. You'll get stuck examining and berating yourself instead of looking outwards, seeing what's really in front of you, and taking steps around, under, over, and through the obstacle. Everything that happens in your life is an opportunity to recalibrate and change your perspective.

Remember a time when you failed to meet some goal and you assumed it was because you were broken or flawed. Maybe there's something inside you that you need to look at and heal—it's not a flaw but a chance for growth. Have a constructive conversation with yourself and start to see where you can offer yourself more love, acceptance, learning, compassion, and perspective. That way you can liberate yourself from the judgment of past experiences; these might be blocking you from having fulfilling experiences now.

If you're still holding on to judgments about a relationship that didn't work out, for example, you may want to work on some self-forgiveness. See the relationship for what it was, what it taught you about your preferences and how you want to be loved. Do your inner work so your next relationship can be deeper and more fulfilling. Instead of dismissing all relationships as hard and impossible, thinking there's something unlovable about you or something wrong with the way you love, keep refining, clarifying, and holding the vision of obtaining what you want. Be specific about the experience of love you want to have.

The same principle applies when you think about how your parents were with you and each other. Forgive yourself and them. Know that they did the best they could and their behavior had nothing to do with you. Don't let your childhood hold you captive.

Sometimes moving on requires a period of grieving and purging. That's okay, but put a deadline on this, so you can let life come back in. Open the shutters and the light will fill you, and you'll see your new direction.

GUIDED MEDITATION

Sit comfortably in a quiet place. Start inhaling and exhaling. Observe the rising and falling of your breath. Center yourself in your heart and come into a still, peaceful place inside of you. Start looking back on your life, through your child-hood, going to school, becoming an adult, being in relation-ships and friendships, your work, and start to track times when things didn't work out. When you felt inadequate and may have felt like you were "less than" others. When you started to build the belief that something was wrong with you because you were different and maybe you didn't fit in, or because you didn't succeed in the way you wanted to. And you told yourself that there was something wrong with you. Take that thought into your heart and look at how erroneous that belief is. Look at how this lie costs your en-ergy, your loving, your light. Start to really accept the truth and the fact that there is nothing wrong with you. That you are whole, you are complete, you are unique, you have all the resources that you need to keep going right now. Tell yourself, "I forgive myself for judging myself for think-ing that there was something wrong with me." Bring this memory in your consciousness and release it, erase it, for-give it. Do this as many times as you need to return to your natural joy—the joy that is stored in your heart and in your soul—and tell yourself, "I'm okay. I'm more than okay. I am wonderful. Whether things work out or don't, nothing can take away my loving, my joy, or my gratitude." Bless all of these experiences, like little stepping-stones, that lead you to your love castle. When you look back now, see the track behind you, all clear, sparkling, and renewed. Take this track and put it in front of you—it's a clear track, it's filled with your light, it is guided, it has your blueprint in it, and it is set with love—and affirm in yourself, "I am moving forward with the absolute knowledge that I am guided and seeing with clarity and illumination. My path is bright before me." Bring as much of this light to your heart, your being, as you can. It's time to give birth to the new belief that there is nothing wrong with you. There is everything right with you, and you are learning and growing from every experience. Now take a deep breath and align yourself with your heart, and fill your lungs with your breath and let this new surge of energy go into your brain and throughout your whole body and feel renewed. Smile inside and out and let this smile radiate and fill you with joy!

7.

KNOW YOUR LINCHPIN

linch·pin: 'lin(t)Shpin / *noun*
A pin passed through the end of an axle to keep a wheel in position.

I was visiting with my beloved friend Joan one Sunday morning, and I was sharing with her how I had been feeling out of sorts for a few days. Without hesitation she asked, "Have you been working out?" I said, "Well, it's been challenging to find my motivation. I've been so focused writing this new book and I've only been working out sporadically." She turned to me and said, "For you, working out is your linchpin."

A linchpin is what keeps the wheel going. Joan was absolutely right. When I go to the gym and even just do cardio for thirty minutes, I leave feeling energized. The shift is dramatic. There's no question that for me, cardio exercise (spinning, elliptical, running on the treadmill, or hiking outdoors) is an emotional, invigorating experience. It connects me back to myself. Walking and yoga are both wonderful, but they're not my linchpin. I need to push my muscles. I'm an "endomorph," so I need to work out my muscles in order to connect with my body. (You can find quizzes online to tell you your body type. That'll give you a hint as to what your body requires.) For me, cardio needs to be a habit, like brushing my teeth.

My sister's linchpin is sleep. She is ruthless about getting eight hours of sleep because that keeps her wheels turning. If she misses that, she starts to feel off balance.

So, I ask you, "What is your linchpin?" Is your linchpin singing, knitting, dancing, time alone, meditating, baking, gardening, throwing the ball around, practicing your breathing exercises, biking, hiking, playing with your dog? There's no one universal linchpin, although all these activities bring you back to your joy and make you feel connected. Sticking to your practice can keep your mind from becoming sluggish, confused, frustrated, unclear, irritated, overwhelmed. Your linchpin returns you to a place of joy, clarity, and productivity. If we return to that space where our wheel connects, everything transforms.

What can you do to make sure you stick to your linchpin no matter what life throws at you? Make it a priority to honor your linchpin; it will energize, rejuvenate, and connect you to your mental, emotional, physical, and spiritual well-being. It's the "pin" that keeps the axle of your wheel in balance, and it lets everything else fall into place.

If you don't know your linchpin, the guided meditation at the end of this chapter will point you to it. Ask your friends about their linchpins. You might already have an inkling what yours is. Once you find your linchpin, ask a buddy to support you for thirty-two days in your new habit, anchoring it, and know that this is your foundation and it's nonnegotiable—it will do wonders for you. It is imperative not to delay or miss a day of doing what is key to your well-being. So anchor the habit. It is believed that it takes twenty-one to twenty-eight days to form a new habit; however, in my personal experience I have found that practicing something consistently for thirty-two days established a new habit.

GUIDED MEDITATION

Take a deep breath and exhale. Be present in your heart. Think of something in your life that makes you feel alive, happy, energized, and connected. What activity is it that when you do it, it shifts everything else in your life? Bring it forward in your creative imagination and imagine yourself doing it. Is it something you need to do every day? A few times a week? How often do you need to do this one thing so you stay on track? When you have it vividly in your imagination, decide how you're going to support yourself to do this activity so you'll stay true to yourself. Make a commitment that for thirty-two consecutive days you will support yourself in doing this one thing that is your "linchpin." Is there someone who can support you in this new commitment? When life gets too busy and too many things are demanded of you and your energy, this support will help you stay true to this one thing that will make everything else fall into place. Repeat this positive statement: "I give myself permission to do the thing that I need to do every day to keep me connected, energized, and recharged. It is now easy for me to practice this habit that makes me experience my joy and my aliveness and fills me with ease and grace." Take a deep breath, and when you open your eyes, know how wonderful it is that you've made this commitment to yourself. Take your journal and jot down what you discovered in this short meditation, and how you're going to support yourself moving forward.

8.

ALLOW YOUR TIMING

Rivers know this: there is no hurry.
We shall get there some day.

—A.A. Milne, *Winnie-the-Pooh*

There is so much pressure in our world to get to what's next. People ask kids who are barely in high school, "What do you want to be when you grow up?" In college, the first question is "What is your major?" When it comes to love, we always feel pressure to meet "the one," and if you're a woman, your biological clock starts to tick tick tick. This pressure we put on ourselves to get somewhere, to become somebody, to have someone love us creates a sense of urgency that obscures our innate wisdom, which would naturally guide the timing of our lives.

I was a late bloomer, and very often I would succumb to the pressure of feeling that I had to catch up. I spent a lot of time worrying that I wasn't finding the true form of expression, my vocation, and the right relationship. It wasn't until later in my life that I realized the years I spent on my inner growth were clearing the pathway to my life's work. Those years of work gave me something to say; I had a contribution to make. I started to experience a sense of fulfillment that didn't come from rushing to advance my career, but from a lot of inner work to really connect with and know myself and what I was here to do.

I love these lines from the third chapter of Ecclesiastes: "To every thing there is a season, and a time to every purpose under the heavens . . . a time to weep, and a time to laugh . . . a time to rend, and a time to sew; a time to keep silent, and a time to speak." These verses hold the wisdom of the cyclical energy of life. Urgency is everywhere, but you need to ask yourself, "Am I honoring my divine timing?" Know that it's never too late. I know people who changed careers in their fifties and started a new vocation; I had a friend who adopted her first child from China at age fifty; I have friends who found true love at sixty-two; I know a woman who started singing when she was fifty-five and made an album.

We're always feeling this push to get *there* faster than everyone else. We see where others are, compare ourselves, think that we should catch up, but never make it and judge our own flow and timing. We live in a society where faster is better, and it makes us lose perspective on how much value there is in taking our time and relishing the moments. This is where the wisdom of our soul and society reside. So find your pace, trust it, and honor it.

How many times have you heard a parent say, "My kid is great, but he hasn't yet found what he wants to do. He's tried three or four things but hasn't really landed on anything substantial." The parent feels bad and this makes the child feel worse. Or you've heard, "She's thirty-two and she's still single." As if this is some Greek tragedy! Comparing our kids to everyone else makes them feel like they're failing, inadequate, like they'll never amount to anything in the future. Give them permission to define their own success, what *their* "good life" is, and let it happen in its own time.

It takes bravery to make up your own rules and map out your own journey, one that will look different from others' journeys. This is a good thing. Don't think that not yet having achieved something means that the door has closed. No more negative self-fulfilling prophecies. Always stay hopeful and know that all your possibilities and opportunities continue to be available to you as you continue on your journey.

The stoic philosophers knew to let the timing of the universe run its course; they never imposed a deadline on the universe. They adopted the philosophy "I don't know *when* I'm going to find what I'm looking for, but I know I will." Remind yourself, "I don't know when I'm going to meet 'the one,' but I know I will." Then get on with life trusting the universe to provide for you. This applies to everything you desire. It doesn't mean that you stop doing, engaging, pursuing, participating, but it does mean that you stop pressuring yourself, calling yourself a failure, and causing yourself a lot of suffering.

When you have an optimistic outlook, you will be a winner in life. Your thoughts create your reality. So think happy thoughts and possibilities, opportunities, and true love will come your way as you maintain a positive inner vision.

If we vibrate with a "YES" to life, the divine will provide in its own perfect time.

GUIDED MEDITATION

This is a guided meditation to tap into your wisdom, patience, and knowledge that everything in your life is moving according to the perfect plan. Come into a comfortable, relaxed position and attune yourself to your breath. Look at the areas of your life where you would like things to go fast. Really ask and access the wiser part of you and see where it is that you're placing pressure on yourself to make things different. Bring your heart present in this moment and accept that at this moment, things are perfect just the way they are. Take your time and do everything you do, but slow down in such a way that you relish and cherish everything that is going on in your life. In being present at every moment, fully participating in your life as it is, you'll be able to unfold to the next chapter of your life and honor your own timing. Honor the wisdom of life's timing and trust that things are unfolding in the perfect way. Breathe in patience, let go of any pressure inside.

Life is so much more joyful when we don't pressure ourselves and things can happen in a miraculous way, when we don't go against the natural flow of our lives. Move into the depths of gratitude with your whole being, and then place a prayer in your heart about anything you would like to have more of. Anticipate it, see it coming, and know that everything will be there for you as you make this moment as sacred and present as you can. Allow guidance, wisdom, patience, and devotion to come in. Take a deep breath, slowing down the exhalation, take a deep breath and slowing down the inhalation, open your eyes and exhale with a sound. Let things be the way they are, at peace.

9.

WORRY AND THE SOUL

If you are troubled by external circumstances, it is not the circumstances that trouble you, but your own perception of them—and they are in your power to change at any time.

—Marcus Aurelius

One lovely summer evening, I took an Uber to have dinner with a friend, and the first thing she said to me when I arrived was "I was worried about whether everything was okay with you and the Uber."

"Everything's fine. No need to worry," I replied.

To which she answered, "I worry about *everything*."

During our dinner she told me that she is constantly worried and frightened that something is going to happen to the people in her life. "I live in a perpetual state of anxiety," she said. "I worry that if my sister doesn't pick up when I call, something has happened to her. When I see my mother is calling me, I worry that she is calling to say that she's fallen. I never imagine good news."

I was absolutely stunned, because I consider my friend a rather evolved human being. "What a way to live. Let's fix that," I said. When I inquired further, she said, "When I was six, my mother left for Europe for a long time, leaving me with my grandmother, and I never knew when she would return. Although she did return, the instability I felt has never gone away."

I'll share some tools for managing this kind of chronic anxiety later in this chapter. But first, let's talk about the more quotidian forms of anxiety we all know so well—that feeling when you are about to go for a job interview, meet a first date, or give a presentation at work, or when you're waiting for medical results or to hear if your child made it into college or if you got that bank loan. You wish you could calm yourself down, but you're like a cat on a hot tin roof. You're bursting at the seams!

You can learn to manage your inner response to anxiety, pressure, and deadlines. There are techniques and practices that can calm you, that will turn you to your soul for support when you need it. What do I mean by *soul*? To me, the soul is your true essence, your wisest and highest self who loves you unconditionally. Your soul is filled with love, compassion, and caring because that is its nature. The more open you are to the expression of your soul, the more you will feel it moving to support you. Your soul will draw in the people who can help you. It knows what you need, what you want, and where you're going. But how do you get calm enough to connect to the wisdom of your soul in those moments when all you can feel are butterflies?

When you are anxious and worried, you often have an underlying fear that something catastrophic is going to happen. Your body tells your brain that danger is coming. It's time for "fight or flight." For example, let's say you're in the middle of a job interview, and your mind says, "They'll find out that I'm not competent and they won't like me. I'll never get a job!" With so many negative thoughts bombarding your brain, it's hard for your poor "self" to feel good about anything! When you recognize your thoughts spiraling in this way, use these techniques to bring your-self to a calm and positive place: Prayer and Reframing.

Prayer is seriously powerful for fighting anxiety. In deep prayer, your spirit can reach calmness, peace, and trust, and you can reconnect to your soul. Try this prayer: "I surrender my fears and anxieties, and ask that they be replaced with inner calmness and trust."

Another tool that I use a lot is to *reframe my anxiety as excite-ment*. For example, while you're waiting for your friends to ar-rive for dinner and worrying about whether you've remembered who's gluten-free, who's vegetarian, who's allergic to tomatoes, or whether you've cooked enough food, you can reframe your anxiety as excitement and gratitude that friends are coming over, that you have a house to entertain in and food to serve. You can project an energizing and wonderful evening for everybody.

Before a speaking engagement, I get butterflies in my stom-ach, but I know that these butterflies are energy awakening in me because I'm going to share my wisdom with the audience. I always tell myself, "Agapi, these people are just like you. They are going through life just like you. Pour it out, be who you are and they're going to love what you have to say." I also have friends who remind me of this when I need it. And my joy awakens. I've reframed the anxiety and I suddenly feel that I can inspire all these people!

What if your problem is more like that of my friend who's always worried? Chronic stress has a debilitating impact on the body and mind over time. When too much cortisol is released into the body, your immune system is lowered and you are more sus-ceptible to everything from colds to cancer. An overload of stress can eventually cause you to suffer from insomnia, depression, and—guess what?—even more anxiety, worry, and fear! The vicious cycle continues.

So, where does your worry come from? At the root of worry is a lack of trust. Without trust, the world is an unsafe, unstable place, and you don't trust that you can handle what life throws at you. You don't trust that help and resources are available to you. Lack of trust is an unresolved emotional issue that causes you to forget that you have inner tools to help you. Find the root cause of your anxiety and bring it to the light.

In the light, you are no longer a victim of a thought or emotion; it can't have its way with you. Take charge of it, reason with it, give yourself new behaviors, new thoughts, and new feelings. A friend taught me this little tool: Whenever she's anxious, she looks at herself in the mirror and says, "STOP THAT!" and shakes herself free of the fear. Or sing "Don't Worry, Be Happy," when you're anxious. Whenever you need it, give it a try.

I have used these inner tools so much that now it's become second nature. I am going to take you through a guided meditation to help you through the tough experiences that are on your plate, so that no matter what, you know that there is always a calm place available for you to return to.

GUIDED MEDITATION

Find a comfortable location where you won't be interrupted for the next few minutes. Take a deep breath and exhale with a sound, "Ahh." Allow yourself to really let go of what's worrying you, preoccupying you, or making you anxious. This moment is just for you. As you breathe in, ask for the presence of your soul, for your being to be present.

Take a few breaths, consciously connecting with a larger presence within you. Connect with your breath and start to feel a sense of rhythm with your own breath, and feel it slowing down.

Bring into your mind's eye a landscape where you have gone and felt calm. Or a place you've seen in photos where you would love to go. In your imagination, go there right now. Let that quietness infuse you. Imagine that you are sitting overlooking this beautiful landscape. Feel the breeze touching your cheeks, the light from the day brightening you up, and the calmness of the landscape infusing your brain cells, your body, and your emotions. As you take your next breath, amplify this calmness. Amplify this quietness until it penetrates all of your senses. No matter what is going on around you, you feel anchored in your calmness. You are filled with a sense of trust about your life and you see positive outcomes and solutions. You imagine things happening just the way you want them to happen. This fills you with a sense of wonder. With a sense of peace. With a sense that you are not alone. But the presence of your own soul is gently ushering you, and participating in all the events of your life.

You start to experience a contentment and a happiness, knowing that miracles will happen in your life. Anticipating goodness, joy, and wonderful outcomes. Take a deep breath and let it permeate any place in your body where in the past you may have felt worried, anxious, nervous, and see yourself stepping into this new calmness everywhere you go. It walks with you. It's your new state of being. It is your new way of relating to life and all it brings your way. You are anchored in your calmness. Feel it in the soles of your feet, palms, hands, heart, into the belly. Feel it and take a deep breath, saying, "I am grounded in my calmness. I'm anchored in the strength and power of my soul. I am anchored in the truth of who I am. I am safe. I am protected. And I am loved." Take a deep breath and allow this new sense of self to fill you, and when you're ready, open your eyes, wriggle your fingers and toes. Breathe, knowing that your calmness is working for you.

10.

ARE YOU LIVING IN DENIAL?

Denial is a verbal, expressive negation of a reality that makes action impossible.

—Kathy McMahon, clinical psychologist

Denial is a very common coping mechanism. It serves us well at different points in our lives. But it can also undermine the wonderful possibilities that wait for us and numb us from feeling alive. It takes a lot of courage to look at the areas in our lives where we could be living in denial.

The most common expression of denial manifests itself in personal relationships. For example, you're dating someone whom you're very attracted to, they're noncommittal, but you keep waiting, hoping that they will change and commit to you. Or you deny that you're unhappy in a marriage because if you face it, you have to do something about it. Either something has to change, or you have to end the marriage. That's a big, life-altering event. So often if we face what we're denying, we have to make big choices, and sometimes they can be extremely painful and uncomfortable.

You could be in denial about your health. I've seen women

come face-to-face with the fact that they put on twenty-five pounds after maintaining that the cleaners had shrunk their clothes. When they face the truth, they're able to take action. Denial paralyzes us, robs us of our energy, and makes productive next steps impossible, so much so that it feels like we're walking around in a fog. When you face the truth, you feel completely vulnerable and naked, and you can be overwhelmed by the suppressed feelings that you're now facing. You need to be self-supporting, self-loving, and self-forgiving so you take a giant step to handle something you've been denying for years.

It happened to me when I was going through menopause and my body changed by two sizes. I have to tell you that my wake-up call came when I saw pictures from an event. Although I felt great, I saw how my body had changed. It took me years to admit to and accept my new body, but once I did, I set an intention to maintain a healthy, toned, and vital body. I had to let go of the self-judgments and consciously take better care of myself. I felt so much more empowered when I took back control and put myself in the driver's seat!

I had to learn this lesson again as I came to terms with my restless sleep syndrome. My cardiologist suggested that I do a study for sleep apnea—a common disorder in which you have one or more pauses in breathing or shallow breaths while you sleep that leaves you tired in the morning. It took me a few years to silence the voice of denial that said, "I don't have apnea. My fatigue is not a big deal, it will go away" and even go to a doctor—and then once I was diagnosed, it took another year to override the same voice saying, "I'll just lose weight and it'll go away." Finally, I went to see a specialist who gave me a night guard to adjust my jaw alignment and open up my sinuses so I could breathe better. I immediately started to feel more energized when I woke up because I had slept more deeply. Within a few months, my energy dramatically shifted. As my sister, Arianna, an advocate of sleep, says, "We finally change when we become sick and tired of being sick and tired."

Maybe you are thinking, "I'm stuck in this job . . . I'm stuck in this relationship . . . I can't leave until the children are older . . . I'm too old to find love . . . I'll never lose the weight . . . I'll never be out of debt." If that sounds like you, you're denying the multitude of choices and opportunities that are available to you. You need to expand from this contracted state of being. You are way more resourceful than that. Help and solutions are available to you, both internally and externally.

Are you afraid to be capable, strong, and dynamic? Why do you deny your power? Is it because you want to belong or hesitate to be in the frontline? Are you afraid no one will love you if you're independent? Do you crave protection and loving, and are you afraid you won't get it if you're strong? In owning our power, we have no more excuses not to have what we really want.

When you've let go of denial, you can experience living in the present moment and finding solutions to your problems. Your wisdom is always informing you of what's going on in your life. Tap into your courage, follow it, trust it, honor it, and know that this true wisdom will guide you to new beginnings.

SUGGESTIONS FOR THIS WEEK

1. Take this week and review your life. Are there any areas you've been avoiding or that stress you out when you think about them? Pick one area. It could range from cleaning your closet, to examining your finances, to that difficult conversation you've been avoiding. Write down in your journal the

worst-case scenario. Become conscious of it, familiarize your-self with this fear. Now, write down the best-case scenario and focus on making this happen. Know that you have the power and resources to face something you've been avoiding.

2. Is there a part of you that's discounting your good attributes— your humor, resourcefulness, openness, thoughtfulness, and how much fun you are? Take time to write down in your jour-nal all the good things about you, claim them, and bring them home to you.

3. Is there a negative self-image you're holding on to that's mak-ing you believe you are worth less than you truly are? This may be cutting off your happiness. Take some time this week to re-flect and write down what you struggle with. Challenge those images and replace them with actions that support the truth of who you are.

11.

OVERCOMING YOUR CHILDHOOD

I am not what happened to me, I am what I choose to become.

—Carl Jung

At some point, we all have to overcome our childhood in order to get on with our life. It's the most important journey we can take that will shape who we become.

One day, a dear friend was sharing with me all of his childhood hurts. When I asked him how he overcame all these struggles, he shared his wisdom: "You're not responsible for what happens to you as a child, but you're responsible to heal it as an adult." When we look back on our childhood, many of us have happy, sweet memories, but sometimes there are other memories that have caused us hurt, pain, and even trauma. Whatever kind of childhood we had, at some point in our adult life, we must have the courage to examine it, see how it has affected us, learn from it, forgive it, and move on. The "moving through" is crucial to our well-being and maturation.

Do you believe in such a thing as the "perfect parent"? Maybe in fairy tales. But in this human world, everybody's got their issues. Even the best parents have their own conditioning, beliefs, and hurts.

In order to overcome our childhood, we need to know where we come from. We need to understand what our parents experienced to make them who they are. Understanding what they went through is important so we can open our hearts to them, forgive what needs to be forgiven, and have compassion.

I loved my parents very much, and they loved and cherished me. My father was a brilliant man who excelled in economics, journalism, and finance and had a powerful presence that commanded a lot of attention. He also carried a lot of pain with him, having been captured by the Germans who occupied Athens, placed in a concentration camp at the age of twenty-five, and held for eighteen months. He survived. But he carried with him the unbearable wound of cruelty inflicted on one human to another during war. My mother was a brilliant woman in her own right with an indomitable spirit who served in World War II with the Red Cross. When they met after the war, they fell madly in love, and their mutual experiences and survivorship deeply bonded them. My father so relished his freedom after being imprisoned that when my mother became pregnant with my sister, he was very reluctant to commit. But he succumbed, they got married, my sister was born, and then began my father's rebellious behavior. He felt trapped in the marriage, so he started to "act out" and have affairs. When my mother became pregnant with me she wanted to abort me, but my father asked her to keep me, so here I am. I had a soul bond with my father that was profound. Even at a young age, I could feel his suffering and did everything I could to bring him joy, comfort, and soothing. He adored me and called me his "comforter." When my mother couldn't endure his infidelities, erratic behavior, gambling, and overspending, she decided to leave. This left her with a deep heartache because she still loved him deeply. When she left and took us away, I felt like the light went out. I was overwhelmed with sadness, missed my father terribly, and could feel his pain more deeply because now we were all separated. I also felt my mother's heartache but didn't know what to do with it. I felt powerless, longed to bring them back together, and so wished I could heal the hurt.

But their hurt wasn't what I needed to heal. As I embarked on my inner journey, I realized what I needed to heal was the unanswered question of how a love so big, between my parents, could go so wrong and cause so much pain. I knew, all the while, that they really loved each other. Why did I have to witness this pain of seeing their hearts shut down to each other? It took me years to realize that their love never left. As my father survived the camps and my mother survived his infidelities, I survived bearing the burden of their pain. I finally saw and understood that whatever we go through, we survive. Love survives.

My parents are now deceased. Before he passed, I witnessed my father ask my mother for forgiveness, tears streaming down his face. Maybe they had to go through all that tumult to reach that glorious moment, to open up to each other again and finally be free. It was a powerful moment that I'll never forget—it brought healing to all of us.

The truth is, you don't really know what each soul has come here to work out, and your job is not to judge, blame, condemn, or heal. Your job is to look at your own journey and serve the purpose of what your soul is here to learn. Once I became clear about my own journey, I knew that I had the right to be happy and joyful, and not be responsible for anyone else's healing.

Maybe you had the best parents in the world, but now you

feel like you can't measure up to the example they set. Maybe your brother or sister got more attention than you, maybe your mom was depressed or a narcissist or your dad was a bully or an alcoholic, or maybe your parents separated like mine. Dysfunctional families come in all shapes and sizes. You can use this as an excuse to shut down and blame everything that goes wrong in your life on your challenging childhood, or you can "choose to become what you want" as Carl Jung tells us.

It's not easy to overcome your childhood, I know. As kids, we all need to feel safe, we need to live in an environment that nurtures us and cultivates our talents, our uniqueness. We need to be validated. Above all, we need to know we are loved unconditionally. A handful of people actually had that kind of childhood. Then there's the rest of us.

What if everything that happened in our childhood was perfectly designed to help us grow, evolve, and learn about ourselves? Believing this takes us away from being a victim and allows us to embrace our power. So don't be afraid. Dig deep and see what you need to learn. What do you need to keep or let go in order to live your own true narrative?

The process of letting go and accepting our parents and our childhood as they are is one of the most profound things we can do for own transformation. Loving, forgiving, and understanding your parents can be one of the greatest awakenings of your life. Your whole life is an education, and your parents are two of the most valuable teachers, no matter who they are and what they did. The day you see that and start to choose what to learn from them, you will feel empowered and free. Healing will begin, and you will know that love not only survives, but triumphs.

SUGGESTIONS FOR THIS WEEK

1. For the next week—and this can go on for as many weeks as you want—make a list of all the things that you're grateful for that your mother and father gave you. Then make a list of all the things you wish you received from your parents but didn't get. Start to see your childhood with deeper understanding and compassion, and see if there is a hidden blessing underneath the difficulties.

2. Connect with the child in you and converse with him or her about any feeling that is still unexpressed about your parents. If there is hurt, disappointment, wishful thinking, or unexpressed love, write a letter to your mother and your father and write a letter to yourself from your higher self-perspective—as if you were the parent of that little boy or girl—listening to yourself and giving yourself the love and compassion you might not have gotten from your parents.

3. Find a picture of yourself as a little boy or girl, and a picture of your parents, and for the next month send loving thoughts and energy to yourself and them daily. This is a powerful way to heal your inner family. Find a place in you that is so loving, so compassionate, so understanding, and open your heart to your inner child and the parents who raised you.

4. If you are one of those people who had loving and wonderful parents, and you feel you would like to express your gratitude and appreciation, there is nothing like giving of your time and presence. Calling, texting, and flowers are wonderful. But quality time with you is the greatest gift you can give back. So find things you and your parents can do together that are

uplifting, joyful, and energizing. You will have these moments to cherish for all time.

GUIDED MEDITATION

We are going to go on a little journey to heal inner blocks from your childhood. Evoke an inner light to fill you, protect you, surround you, and assist you right now in clearing anything you don't want to hold on to anymore. So often we shape beliefs about ourselves in our childhood that restrict the beauty and the power of who we are right now. We are now going to give ourselves permission to see these beliefs and release them.

Have you read fairy tales featuring wonderful fairy godmothers? Right now, take a deep breath, exhale, and imagine the most wonderful fairy godmother, dressed to the nines, coming to visit you. She takes you down memory lane to when you were a child. She's holding your hand, and you are looking into your childhood. See yourself with your parents at your childhood home and describe to yourself how you felt. Was there enough love for you? Was it peaceful at your home? Were there siblings, extended family? Was there something you would like to have been different? Was there pain, separation, yelling, strict orders? What was the environment like? Just see it, as if you were watching a movie.

As you go through all these memories, place your right hand on your belly and take this child to your heart, and let this child speak to you. What would he or she like to have been different? Let this child tell you his or her desires.

How was school, the classmates, the first love, separation or closeness with your friends, thinking that other kids had more? The worries of growing up. See it all with compassion, with acceptance. Are there any areas you can move into with forgiveness? Forgiving your parents for not having done more for you. For being who they were. They did the best they could. Just forgive them. Forgive yourself for any pain or hurt or thinking that you weren't good enough. Just forgive it and let it go.

Your fairy godmother is sitting right here, and she gives you a magic wand. Take it in your hand, take this power in your wand and shake it into every area of your childhood and tell yourself, "I have the power to let go of all this, I can bless it and let it go. I am way more than my childhood, and I can now forgive and let go of any memories that were not happy for me." Rewrite the now the way you want to. Because right now you can create an entire, new bright story for yourself. Is there anything you need to do to complete your childhood so you can upgrade yourself to being a healthy, wonderful, responsible adult? Extend your love to your family, your compassion to yourself. It's not easy growing up, it never is for anyone. With few exceptions, most of us didn't have ideal childhoods. So give yourself permission to let go, to forgive, and to love.

When you are ready, open your eyes, take a sip of water, and write in your journal anything you need to write to release memories and judgments and replace them with a feeling of goodness and gratitude for your life.

12.

LONGING AND PROLONGING

Beware of destination addiction, the idea that happiness is in the next place, the next job, or even with the next partner. Until you give up the idea that happiness is somewhere else, it will never be where you are.

—Author unknown

I have been caught in cycles of longing many times. Different kinds of longings, too. I longed to express myself in acting, in work that fulfilled me and gave me joy. But one that cycled over and over again is romantic longing. Wanting to be locked in a lover's arms, gazing into each other's eyes, feeling the rapture of love. You know the kind of thing I mean; like the stuff you read in Nicholas Sparks's books.

I have had my share of falling in love and being consumed with thoughts of another person over the years. When I didn't have it, I so wanted it. What's the "it" I wanted? A loving relationship, sure, but I also had a fantasy of what that should look like. If you err on the side of "fantasy" in your relationship seeking, it can lead to addictive pursuit and borderline obsession with your love object because you're pursuing something that doesn't actually exist. This will never give you the happiness you seek, and those relationships never last. But I totally get it. Our culture promotes "love" in a way that makes it hard to have a good grasp on what real love actually is in practice.

When I was researching the Greek goddesses, specifically Aphrodite and her son Eros, I dove into literature to find examples of the kind of passionate, erotic love that Aphrodite embodies. I watched a movie called *Dangerous Beauty* based on the true story of Veronica Franco, a Venetian courtesan from the sixteenth century who was also a well-known poet. As a courtesan, she was the very essence of Aphrodite: beautiful, free in love-making, charming, seductive. Every man fell in love with her. Because of her feminine power, she was brought before the Spanish Inquisition and tried as a witch. Most of the men prosecuting her were also patrons—and so she was acquitted. Watching the film, I swooned at the love scenes and even memorized the speech she made in front of her prosecutors: "I confess I became a courtesan, traded yearning for power, welcomed many rather than be owned by one." That kind of passion and abandon is something I found myself craving over the years.

There was a time in my life when I was touched by that aphrodisiac kind of love. When I was with that person, the world ceased to exist. But the relationship was also very dysfunctional and complicated; at some point, it started to cause more pain than pleasure. One day, we would be completely immersed and enjoying one another, feeling totally in love and connected. Then suddenly he would retreat and disconnect, withdrawing his love. Then he'd show up again, as if nothing had happened, and want to pick up where we left off. It was all because of his fear of intimacy. I knew I should have ended it sooner than I did, but I was hoping he would get over his fears. Being in this relationship wasn't easy. It all came to a head after we returned from a holiday. He withdrew his loving yet again, and I was finally done.

My first step in separating from him was telling him it was over and reinforcing that by not taking his calls or answering texts. Extricating myself from someone who had gotten under my skin was a deep process. I decided to choose me and my well-being over a relationship that caused me pain and unhappiness. It felt like I had walked so deeply into the ocean and I had to retreat back to the shore, shake myself out, and find my footing. It became one of the greatest journeys of self-discovery. It awakened a lot of compassion in me for others caught in this kind of dysfunctional and addictive attachment.

The day that I decided to let go of the relationship, I prayed with all my might and asked for inner support. I heard in a clear voice, from my inner guides, "We will help you, but you mustn't see or interact with him because then you'll be pulled back into the relationship." So I pulled all my energy back into myself by going to dance and improvisation classes, keeping active, hanging out with uplifting friends, writing in my journal, and meditating. My heart was in pain from the separation. But I kept filling the emptiness with new projects and continuously asked for help. The wise guidance I received to not interact or engage with him was the key to getting free.

If you have ever been in a situation like this, or you're in it now—where you want to be free of longing or of a relationship that is no longer working for you—be very strategic about finding new ways to express yourself. Make sure that you have loving, supportive members of your tribe around you, helping you through your process. All your energy has been invested in that relationship and it needs new places to go.

It took approximately nine to twelve months for me to regain my complete self and recenter. That kind of connection with another person can awaken something inside you that's so beautiful, so alive; it feels as though you can't access that aliveness on your own. However, that's not true. That feeling is yours. Your joy, beauty, and loving are all yours and you must find ways to conjure them on your own. As you let go of a relationship and start to take steps on your own, I know you can cross the bridge to the other side, where your own fullness awaits you.

The journey to real love has nothing to do with fantasies, wishful thinking, or denial; instead, it encompasses all the aspects of yourself and the one you are with. It requires a profound commitment to truth and going the distance together. Keep in mind that the best relationships are a ménage à trois: you, the other person, and spirit.

SUGGESTIONS FOR THIS WEEK

1. When you decide you want to let go of a romantic relationship full of longing, make a commitment to yourself that for the next thirty-two days you will start directing your energies and your focus into the things that spark your joy and creativity. Start to write in your journal what these things are. They could be cooking, singing, painting, dancing, crafting, learning a language, writing, playing soccer, starting a book club, working on your business plan—so many things for you to do!

2. Find one or two friends who will hold and support you in this new direction. Ask them to be there as your allies, helping you redirect your focus by doing things that are new, creative, and supportive.

3. Travel. For the next month, find new places around your own neighborhood or go to a different city or country, to a new

place where you interact with new people, environments, and language and replace old pictures with new images that will give you a new perspective. By immersing yourself in another culture, you can be invigorated in a way you've never experienced.

13.

HOW TO LET LOVE IN

Embark on the Journey of Love. It takes you from yourself to your Self.

—Rumi

Have you ever been betrayed? A lover's infidelity, a friend's rejection when you needed her most, your parents' failure to accept you as you are, or by life itself. What happens then? I know what I've done: I've continued on with my life, but with some big barriers erected between me and the world. I've barricaded myself. The easy advice is to just "move on," and most of us do move on, we go on living our lives. But do we keep our hearts open? That's the really hard part in the wake of betrayal.

How can you forgive and regain your belief that love survives and is yours to have? Be comforted by the fact that you are bigger than the pain. Love is more powerful than hurt.

When my parents separated, my father, in his deep pain, cut off his communication with me, withdrew his affection. He never stopped loving me, but he couldn't express it. This caused me a lot of pain and led me to mistrust love. It showed me that love can be conditional and there's always a risk that it can be taken away. Because of this childhood experience, I had a fear that if I let love in, especially from a man, I would become dependent upon him and maybe then that love would be taken away. I felt much safer pushing love away instead.

But I paid a big price for this caution. It was like looking at the beautiful, warm, inviting Aegean Sea, longing to dive in but refusing to dip my toe. I had to do a lot of healing work to open up, trust, and let love in again.

It took me a while to understand that people don't always love us the way we want. They love us the way they can love us. I often experienced a sense of frustration or resistance to how someone loved me and how it was expressed, so I would shut down.

It helped me to read *The Five Love Languages* by Dr. Gary Chapman, a book that teaches you which of the five languages of love you prioritize, how to communicate your needs, and how to understand and accept and return your partner's love. Maybe you perceive love through words of affirmation, or for you it's a loving touch. Maybe you know you're loved when you receive a thoughtful gift or when your partner performs an act that makes your life easier.

For me, quality time together is most important. I personally *love* to stay connected to the people in my life. I call, e-mail, text, and always prioritize spending time with them. My younger niece, Isabella, is an introvert. I know how much she loves me and I love her unconditionally, but if we go for a long period of time without spending quality time together, I crave her company. So I tell her how much spending time together means to me. We make it a priority. Remembering that we all have different love languages keeps you from spiraling into catastrophic thinking when you experience a blip in your relationship.

One of the most pivotal moments in this journey, where everything clicked, was when my spiritual teacher, John-Roger, hugged me and held me close to his heart and said, "Let the love in. There is pain there, but underneath the pain there is beauty, tenderness, and your heart. Don't be afraid." I started to weep. The pain I still carried from my father's withdrawal of love started to release.

Sometimes it feels like the most difficult thing to do is to let our *own* loving in. When I moved to New York City to write my first book, away from my family, it was very difficult to adjust. I missed them, feeling lonely and isolated. I had been used to being loved by others, and I didn't know how to truly love myself. One night, I told my best friend how lonely I felt, and she responded, "Why? You are with my favorite person in the world . . . YOU." This made me laugh. I was her favorite person, but I wasn't my own favorite person. I *wanted* to become my favorite person. It took a long time to truly become comfortable with myself and enjoy my aloneness—to let my own love in. I was conditioned to experience my own aliveness by being with others. When you open the channels to your own loving, and live in its fullness, then you're not always dependent on other people's love toward you to fill your cup.

When I gradually learned to release the barriers to my own loving and let in my own sweetness and self-love, it was much easier to see the ways in which other people loved me. I allowed the sweetness and depth of their love to come in, regardless of what it looked like.

There have been times when I've sat in a park watching the children playing, the younger teens kissing, the older people strolling with their canes, and people chatting—and suddenly, it looks like the playground of love. When you catch that essence underneath these everyday interactions and let it in, it feels like the curtain lifts on how you perceive the world, the harshness of separation melts, your heart softens, and you start to reside in the presence of love. This takes a willingness to be vulnerable, open, and tender. Back away from the demands you place on love and release your expectation of what love should look like, and you will experience the essence of who you are. That's how you let love in. In the profound stillness of acceptance, you will realize that love has never left you.

GUIDED MEDITATION

Sit comfortably in a chair where you know you won't be interrupted for a little while, and attune yourself to your breath. Slow down your breathing. As you inhale and exhale, allow yourself to be still, quiet, calm, and present. Soften your heart and bring it into the present. Let go of your thoughts, relax your mind and your body. Let the tensions go, any worries, or any decisions you've made about love and your worthiness to receive it. Be very present with the miracle of your breath. As you breathe in, this time bring in your consciousness—the awareness of love. Whatever love is for you, whether you've experienced it recently, a long time ago, or it's present for you now, it doesn't matter. Bring up what love is in you right now—whatever that love feels like to you: kind, patient, caring, tender, joyful— fill yourself with that feeling and see yourself softening inside. Smile, a faint, beautiful inner and outer smile and tell yourself, "Ahh, I am letting love in. I am letting love in. I am letting love in. I am safe to let love in." As you open your heart, imagine that there is a wave of love, a wave of kindness—no resistance, no fear but a sense of absolute, total safety and protection.

Allow the people in your life to love you the way they love you, and take in their love and caring, taking the love you've experienced, even if you were not the beneficiary of that love but the observer of love. Let that love in. Let it in from things you have read that have moved you, from movies you have seen, from poems you have read, from people in the street, from wherever you have glimpsed it, let the love in and keep lifting any veils that separate you and restrict you from letting love in. As you relax your heart and your whole being, allow yourself to be immersed in a presence of love. Stay there for a few moments . . . quiet, still, present, and full. Read this poem about love by George Herbert:

> Love bade me welcome. Yet my soul drew back
> > Guilty of dust and sin.
> But quick-eyed Love, observing me grow slack
> > From my first entrance in,
> Drew nearer to me, sweetly questioning,
> > If I lacked any thing.
>
> A guest, I answered, worthy to be here:
> > Love said, You shall be he.
> I the unkind, ungrateful? Ah my dear,
> > I cannot look on thee.
> Love took my hand, and smiling did reply,
> > Who made the eyes but I?

Truth Lord, but I have marred them: let my shame
Go where it doth deserve.
And know you not, says Love, who bore the blame?
My dear, then I will serve.
You must sit down, says Love, and taste my meat:
So I did sit and eat.

Whenever you need, read this poem out loud to yourself or your friends as a reminder that love is always welcoming you, unconditionally, to feast at her table.

Whenever you're ready, take both of your hands and place them over your heart, and anchor that feeling of letting love in. Take a deep breath, and as you exhale, open your eyes, wriggle your fingers and toes, roll your neck to the left and right, and with that feeling of having let love in, experience the openness and fullness of your heart. As you come present back in the room, stay open and receptive to love.

14

SO, YOU WANT TO GET MARRIED

We come to love not by finding a perfect person, but by learning to see an imperfect person perfectly.

—Sam Keen

As a young girl, I loved going out to the movies with my family, and so many of the films would end with the leading actor and actress getting married. The film would finish with "The End." So I assumed that when people got married, it was the end of the story. My parents' marriage taught me that the end didn't mean a *happy* ending—more like unhappily ever after. I didn't want to get married. During my teenage years, I would pass by my local church, see couples getting married, and think to myself, "I hope this never happens to me." I thought marriage was "the end" for them—and not in a good way. As life went on, though, I yearned to be in an unconditionally loving relationship, and I thought the way to get that kind of relationship was to get married. I had various relationships as a young woman but could never seem to find "the one."

After drama school, I moved from London to L.A., where I met and fell madly in love with an actor. And he fell in love with me. We had a beautiful love affair, romantic and fun, but at some point it ended.

Years later, I was asked to perform in a play called *Love Letters* by A. R. Gurney. We were looking for somebody to play the leading male role opposite me. A friend suggested that I ask my ex-boyfriend to play the role. I hadn't seen him in years but that idea sounded genius to me! I called him, offered him the role, and he accepted. It was great reconnecting and performing together for a few weeks.

We had dinner one night to catch up. We talked about his children and the challenges of his marriage. I revealed to him, "After we broke up, I was married for a short while. It didn't really work out and I never got married again." He looked at me and said in a very matter-of-fact way, "That was never your dream." It hit me like a thunderbolt: How did he know that, when I didn't even know it myself? I asked him how he knew and he said, "When we were together, I felt that marriage wasn't something you ever longed for."

I went home and reflected on the truth of his statement. I had thought I wanted to get married, but no, that's what my parents wanted, that's what society sets as the baseline for normal. At some point, we are expected to find our life partner to love, to start a family and share life with that person. But that wasn't my truth.

Over the years, I went through various relationships, but what I thought I really wanted never came together in one person. I watched many friends find love and overcome challenges, others marry and divorce, others remain happily married after forty years. I saw every form and dynamic of "love." And I kept looking for my perfect match.

The turning point for me came when I was dating a man in New York. I had once again picked a man who was emotionally unavailable, and I got wrapped up in him, losing my sense of myself. My primary focus in life was that relationship. I really thought he was "the one." But it didn't work out. So there I was again; I had created a relationship with an end, consistent with my childlike belief that relationships meant "the end" and there was no "happily ever after." That's when something shifted in me. I decided to take a sabbatical from men and get honest with myself about what I truly wanted.

Shortly thereafter, it dawned on me that my perfect love never manifested because I was ambivalent about it. When I looked more deeply into myself, I realized that what I really wanted was to know myself, be there for myself, to connect with my soul, and to find and express the calling of my life. Somewhere in me, I knew that was where I'd find my fulfillment. Not in another, but in me. In pulling all my energies inward and finding the power in being "singular," I experienced the fullness of expression that I truly wanted for myself.

Each one of us has an individual path that we need to honor, whether that's one we travel alone or with a committed partner. There are many ways to have a relationship, and it's so important not to judge anyone's expression of love.

Often when a relationship doesn't work out, we feel as though we have failed, or that love has failed, and resolve that next time we won't let love in. This can cause a lot of pain. And it's just not true—there is no failed relationship. Relationships are our greatest teacher because they help us grow as individuals, teach us to love unconditionally, show us how to trust ourselves and others, and help us evolve.

Ultimately, the only relationship you are in control of is the one with yourself. Enrich that relationship as much as you can. It's a true joy. It really comes back to getting to know you, getting to love you, and then sharing that love with whomever crosses your path. And if you still want to get married? That's awesome. But marry yourself first, for better or worse, and then you're bound to have a great relationship with whomever you choose to be with. Instead of "The End," this is your "Grand Beginning."

SUGGESTIONS FOR THIS WEEK

1. Write in your journal an ideal vision of what your life looks like in a relationship. How do you want to feel in this relationship? How do you want to interact? What are values you hope to share? Be clear about them, be open and don't settle. Make sure it's not what your parents want or what society dictates. This is your life. Define what it is that you want.

2. Be wise when you share the intimacy of your heart. Get to know someone really well before you reveal your vulnerable self. So many times we project what we want to see on someone, and that can cloud the reality of who they are. Watch for the signs, be vigilant and smart. Take your time to get to know someone.

3. Don't ever marry (or even date) potential. Don't look at someone and say, "Look at all she/he can be. With my help, they'll get there." People are who they are, and changing them is an illusion. Love someone for who they are now, and if their gifts flourish while you're together, enjoy being a part of that.

4. Watch one of my favorite TED Talks by Tracy McMillan entitled "The Person You Really Need to Marry." Her journey and perspective on marriage are invaluable.

15.

THE GIFT OF INTIMACY

> There is no greater act than putting yourself before another. Not before another as in coming first, but rather as in opening yourself up before another, exposing your essence before another. Only in being this authentic can real kinship be known and real kindness released.
>
> —Mark Nepo

I love the word *intimacy*: in–to me–see. It is one of the greatest gifts we can give to ourselves and each other, and it is what most people long for. We all long to be truly seen and cherished for who we are.

Life without intimacy is dry. When we are intimate, we take our humanness and vulnerability into our hands and expose it. As we show it, we connect with parts of ourselves that we didn't even know were there. We start to experience our essence instead of personality, emotions, or thoughts. That's why people love to fall in love. In that "glow" you see the beauty of who you are; love is awakened in you. This love with another doesn't always last, but you have to keep practicing intimacy to get to the deeper parts of yourself. You can practice intimacy on your own—you don't need a partner. Before you can be intimate with someone else, you first need to be intimate with yourself.

While I was studying spiritual psychology at the University of Santa Monica, I was aware that a lot of suppressed pain had surfaced. So one day after class, I went home and drew a bath. There, in a moment of relaxation, immersed in warm water, I was able to communicate with a part of myself that for years had felt hurt and neglected. This was the little girl in me who felt unexpressed pain after my parents separated. I opened my heart to that part of myself, my little girl, and allowed all of the old tears and pain to come out. It was an exquisitely vulnerable moment, and I was filled with tenderness and gratitude and touched to my core. In that tub, I sent a message to my younger self: "I got you, girl." I started to feel happy and safe.

At that moment, I made a promise to myself to never leave me behind ever again, and I experienced a moment of true inner bonding. I bought myself a ring as a symbol of my restored connection to myself. Every time I put on the ring, I light up inside. Don't leave a part of yourself behind. Take the time to create a space to get to know and embrace the abandoned parts of you.

Once you establish this personal intimacy and feel safe with yourself, it is easier to bring your authentic self to other relationships. We're obviously much more comfortable showing our strengths and bravery to others, but it's way more courageous to open up and show our vulnerabilities and the places that need healing. We all have them. We all could use loving ears and loving hearts to listen to us.

As Doris Lessing said, "Do you know what people really want? Everyone, I mean. Everybody in the world is thinking: I wish there was just one person I could really talk to, who could really understand me, who'd be kind to me. That's what people really want, if they're telling the truth." So why not decide to be that one person for someone else?

My mother used to call it "the human communion," and she had the gift of knowing how to make it happen: she would always give those she was with her full attention, create a space where people could be open and feel safe, and always share her authentic self.

I watched my mother bond with everyone—the FedEx man, the supermarket cashier, the taxi driver, or any human being God put in front of her, regardless of status, job, or wealth. She made it her purpose to not miss the moment. When we would say, "We're in a hurry," she would put up her hand and say, "Darling, don't hurry me. I'm having a precious moment with this person. You can go ahead without me." She meant it, and people in her presence felt like one million dollars because they were the most important thing in her life at that moment. So I have learned from her, and I, too, make it a point to create these intimate moments with others.

When we experience intimacy, our hearts soften and unbind and we start to experience our own humanness, our sense of connection and our sweetness. We often experience intimate moments with babies and small children because they are more open and haven't put up barriers yet.

In the hustle and bustle of our daily life, with thousands of things to complete, including the unpredictable things that come up, it becomes very challenging to focus on intimacy and connection. After all, who has time to stop and connect? Most of our social engagements have an agenda. However, all of our activities and preoccupations can be transformed in a moment of true intimacy with another human being. Time stops and we become fully present with another, and in that moment of authenticity a spark ignites and our truth is seen by another.

To build intimacy, ask others, "What do you struggle with in your life?" I always volunteer what I struggle with to open up the conversation. As a result, I have all of these amazingly intimate encounters, learning about who people really are instead of what they do.

Our hearts communicate so much more without words, and when we give ourselves permission to go to that place in our heart, we experience other people's hearts, and a part us of recognizes and knows them. In this intimate communion, we can feel a oneness, and we capture the sweetness of life.

SUGGESTIONS FOR THIS WEEK

1. Make it your intention every day to experience intimacy. First practice having a few moments with yourself, and allow yourself to become present in your vulnerability. Fill yourself with your own loving, forgiveness, and compassion. As you go about your day, practice silent intimacy, creating interactions where you share authentically and create a safe space for others to do the same.

2. Invite a few friends over and create a space of intimacy. Whether it's during dinner or a support circle, take a candle and pass it around, and as each person holds the candle, he places his heartfelt desires, wishes, or concerns into this circle of safety and intimacy. If you decide to have dinner, invite everyone around the table to share a heartfelt moment with the

group. I have often done this, and everyone has felt enriched and connected.

3. Practice random moments of intimacy: at work with a colleague, with your kids while making dinner, at the coffee counter with the barista, with the cashier at the supermarket, with your elderly parents who need help. When you ask someone, "How are you?" have the intention of listening and letting them know that you really care; there is nothing mechanical about intimacy. Record these moments in your journal and return to them often to see how impactful intimacy can be.

4. Repeat this positive statement to yourself, as often as you need: "I allow intimacy in my life with friends, family, those I meet, and myself."

16.

HEALING THE PAIN OF SEPARATION

The person who finds the spark in himself or herself can believe that everyone has that spark. It will take time for all of us to realize this. But imagine if each of us who has found our spark tries to connect to that spark in everyone we meet.

—Maki Kawamura

I've never met anyone who hasn't dealt with the pain of separation: hurt feelings, unexpressed wishes, blocked communication, alienation, anger. What causes this pain is basic and simple: we turn off the source of our loving. Love is free flowing, like water. Whenever we shut off the flow of our love to others, we suffer, because we have also shut off the flow of love to ourselves.

When my parents separated, I witnessed the pain that resulted when they stopped talking to each other. My father completely shut down, withdrew his love, and we could all feel it. It felt as though I had been swimming in a calm lake on a warm, sunny day, and then all of a sudden the air turned cold and the water frigid. The lake iced over. I felt certain that the warm water was still there, beneath the ice, but I had no idea how to get to it.

I've been on the other side of it, too. I've iced over—closed myself off to someone who wanted to be close. After my parents passed, three and a half months apart, I went through a hard time. I was living in New York on my own, promoting my first book, and feeling tremendous loss, grief, and pain. I felt like I was walking around with both of my arms cut off. One of my friends had fallen in love with the man of her dreams, and they moved in together. She would often invite me to dinner with the two of them. It was very challenging to be in her presence, with the glow of her new love, while I was miserable and grieving. Quite frankly, I didn't know how to communicate that. I was happy for her, but the timing was very bad. So, I avoided communication. When she would call and ask, "Are you okay? Have I done something to upset you?" I would very politely deflect and say, "I'm fine. I'm just grieving." I completely separated myself from my friend and withdrew my loving. I was hurting and I couldn't be vulnerable with her with our lives in different worlds. I put distance between us because I didn't know what else to do.

When I was past the grief and her love moved from honeymoon to seasoned, of course, it was easier to be with her. We moved on and continued to be friends.

The only way to melt the ice is to forgive, whichever side of it you are on. If you want to be liberated from the pain of separation, you have to be willing to forgive over and over again, until it releases. Forgive yourself, the other person, the situation. With my friend, this is what forgiveness looked like: "I forgive myself for judging myself for feeling grief and pain, for judging my friend for feeling so happy. I forgive myself for being disappointed with myself for feeling that way. I forgive myself for being angry at God for giving her what she wanted and taking away from me the people I loved. I forgive myself for judging myself for withdrawing my loving. I give myself permission to feel the way I feel, and for her to feel the way she feels, and to allow time for healing."

If you are on the receiving end of someone shutting you out, or icing you out—it may be friends, family, colleagues, a significant other, a passing acquaintance—forgive yourself for any judgments you are making on yourself. Move into a state of forgiveness with statements like "I forgive myself for judging myself for being upset that this person has shut me out. I forgive myself for judging them for being the way they are. I forgive myself for not understanding why this is going on. I forgive myself for wanting this to be different. I forgive myself for taking on the blame of this situation. I forgive myself for feeling frustrated about not being able to do something about it. I allow this person their process, and I allow myself to stay open regardless and stay in my loving."

It always comes back to being responsible to ourselves and not blaming others for how they are with us. As hard as it may seem, be self-supportive and ask yourself, "What do I need to do to release myself from the judgment and the way I feel so I can go dive back into the warm water?" Releasing yourself from the chain of separation and allowing your loving to flow is one of the greatest gifts you can give yourself. It's worth everything to bask in the warmth of your own loving.

GUIDED MEDITATION

Get into a comfortable position in a place where you won't be interrupted. Exhale. Close your eyes. Let go of any tensions, any restrictions, anything that is holding you back from your own loving. Bring your heart present.

Ask yourself if there's a situation that has been bothering you, something that may be creating separation between you and another. Any miscommunication? Any hurt feelings? Any resistance? Anything you are holding as resentment that's unexpressed and has created a block between you and your heart, that has brought a sense of pressure that is interfering with the natural flow of energy and goodness in your life. Whatever it is, just make it present in your mind and in your heart, right now. Just allow it to be there. It's okay. We all do the best we can in handling these situations. Is there anything you need to forgive? A judgment on yourself? A judgment on someone else? A judgment on a situation? Something you need to forgive so you can be freer inside? If so, would you allow yourself to forgive a judgment you may have placed against yourself that's shutting you off from your heart? Allow yourself to just go there and know that when you soften your heart and let go of the judgment, you don't have to like the other person, you don't have to like the situation, you don't have to agree, but you can move into acceptance and let go of the restriction. That way, you are free.

Imagine your heart softening, and if you are holding something against the other person, find a place inside of you where you can be compassionate. Compassionate for yourself, compassionate for the other person. As you open your heart, see if there is more light that can come in and shine. Release a sense of separation that you have placed between you and this other person. Send her a wave of positive energy. Send her a wave of light. That frees you up from any restrictions you may have been holding against her. Why not send good energy her way? This frees you up to be in your joy, in your openness and in your sense of oneness. People might not change, circumstances might not change, but you will be walking free and without the disturbance and more aligned with your sense of peace, oneness, and calmness.

Ask now for your high self and spirit to intervene and assist you in any way that you can be assisted to resolve this issue that is present and has brought you any disturbance. Just hand it over. You walk free. Here is a wonderful positive statement: "I hand this situation over to the spirit within and I walk free. I hand this problem over to the spirit within and I walk free. I hand this challenge over to the spirit within and I walk free." I think it's wonderful to know that you can walk free from any disturbance and you have a choice and can exercise it. You never know, once you walk free, people change, circumstances change, and problems can disappear and solutions appear. Take all of this goodness in now, into the depths of your heart, bringing more light into your whole body, and feel a sense of balance and connection. When you are ready, take a deep breath, inhale and exhale with a sound, "Ahh." Open your arms, take in all the goodness, and give yourself a big, warm hug. When you're ready, open your eyes, take a sip of water, smile inside and out, and see if there's been a shift inside of you that has made everything look a little brighter.

17

MAKE YOUR EGO YOUR ALLY

If we utilize the ego correctly, we can have it function for us, being aware that as soon as we give our power over to it, it can destroy us. It will destroy us by making us believe we are the ego. It will turn us away from our greater awareness of who we truly are—the Soul.

—John-Roger

It's kind of a shame that the ego gets such a bad rap. Some think having an ego means you're demanding and self-absorbed. However, this is only true if you allow it to be in the driver's seat. You need to have an ego to function in the world; it's your sense of self and how you interact *with* the world. That's the simple truth. The healthier your sense of ego and the more you educate it to serve your higher self, the more you will shepherd it to work for you, rather than against you.

Of course your ego can block you from progressing in your life. If you are so concerned with defending your own position, with being right, that you are no longer able to receive input from others and from new experiences, your ego can absolutely hold you back. Have you ever encountered someone who "knows" everything? Or thinks he does? That's his ego running him. But the more you become aware of yourself as a creator, the more you are anchored in your heart, then the more you can use your ego in service of the world around you.

As a person who wants to be out in the world, you have to have an ego or you won't have the energy to accomplish anything. Egos are our motivators: they get us achieving, exercising, working hard, and accomplishing impossible things. Every athlete who wants to be the best has an ego. Your ego can be your best ally because it will push you forward to try new things, keep you going when in doubt, and make you fearless in pursuing your heart's desires. On the other hand, if your ego is weak, you'll underestimate your own ability, you won't move past obstacles to get what you want, you'll second-guess yourself, you'll give up.

The ego gives you a sense of worthwhileness and self-esteem and makes you dare to try things that require courage. But it judges and criticizes to survive; when it's feeling inferior, it can go to extremes in order to feel superior. You have a responsibility to educate your ego—tell your ego, you don't always have to be number one. You're more powerful when you have compassion and empathy, when you can recognize that your ego is trying to create a competition where there isn't one. A healthy and evolved ego will work with people in a spirit of oneness, lifting up others to their highest potential. Living with this awareness frees you to live with more joy and gratitude.

There are two negative expressions of the ego. An inflated ego can block your progress by filling you with vanity, greed, entitlement, jealousy, impatience, anger, and a generally false sense of self. It demands that you get what it wants at all costs and at the expense of others. This is a sure way to lose yourself and feel absolutely miserable. On the other hand, a deflated ego can allow others to step on you and keep you from defending yourself, your rights, and your truth. Know that humility and a sense of service are not sourced from a deflated ego; they are high qualities of the soul. We need to learn the difference.

In your professional life, whether you work in business, as a teacher, or as a performer or any other kind of creative work, there is a delicate balance between the aspects of the ego. Let's say you're an actor auditioning for a role. You have to show up with a sense of self, confidence, and intention to get the part. You have to assume that you are the best person for the role. On the other hand, you can't walk into auditions or performances with so much bravado and arrogance that you are blocked from being your creative self. The same principles apply when you're interviewing for a job: you have to have enough confidence to show that you're capable and self-sufficient, while also having enough humility to show that you can be of service and a good collaborator with others.

Then there's recognizing the ego in other people, and learning how to respond to that.

For example, when I have received feedback in the past, and the person is speaking from a place of "ego," I have felt criticized and judged, and automatically defended myself. However, if the feedback comes from a place of love and care, I will take the feedback and correct my course. In turn, when giving feedback about how I want things done, if I speak from my ego, I see the other person shut down. However, if I speak from the heart, the other person sees my intentions and implements the changes. It is truly an art learning how to communicate with one another from a place of heart and wisdom, not from a position of criticism and judgment. I want to inspire you to understand how to work with your ego and other people's egos because it is a wonderful tool that can help you achieve a more balanced way of living.

When I came face to face with my ego, I learned one of the most profound lessons in my life. Working as an actress in Los Angeles was a prime opportunity to learn about "the ego."

I had been hired to perform in an unpaid production of *Never on Sunday*, which featured Greek American actors. I was so thrilled to be acting again that it didn't matter at all that I wasn't financially compensated.

The director had what we can politely call "personality issues": tyrannical, opinionated, and a bit of a bully. We were rehearsing outside L.A. at the height of rush hour. My scenes weren't until much later in the night, so I asked if I could come a little later than call time to avoid traffic. The director responded, "I want the whole cast here at four p.m. and if you don't want to come, I can replace you with one of the many people who want to play your part." I so wanted to retaliate, to let her have it. But I didn't want to risk being fired, so I kept quiet. For four weeks, it was one thing after another. After each night's performance, we had to strike the set, and sometimes we also had to clean the bathrooms—not your typical acting assignment. Meanwhile, I had auditioned for a part as a housekeeper in *Surviving Picasso*, starring Anthony Hopkins, and I found out before a performance that I got it! I was so ecstatic that I would be moving on toward this next opportunity that when I had to clean the house seats after the show, I decided to be a joyful cleaner and put my whole heart into it. As I was cleaning, I started to cry. My heart softened, and I felt that my ego was melting away. All the anger and the fury I had at the director transformed to gratitude.

All the ego strings around my heart loosened, allowing my heart to beat with freedom. The air could finally come back in, and I was in my own flow of loving and creativity. My director noticed this shift, and she softened, saying, "Agapi, you have done enough, go out with your friends." Isn't that funny—when I shifted, she shifted. I remember driving home that night with a sense of elation and liberation.

Here's how I handle my ego when it's getting out of balance: I don't judge it. I learn the difference between my ego and my higher wisdom. I have realized that my power lies in not letting my ego get the best of me. In this place of true power, not assumed power, my confidence shows up. The truth inside me speaks, and I let go of my ego's "right and wrong"—I no longer care about winning. I care more about returning to a heartfelt place and connecting with others. So, I choose to trust my heart and let it shine through with its light and strength, and witness the extraordinary ability it has to transform every situation and relationship.

People's egos will always exist: retaliating, fighting, competing, arguing, holding on to disappointment, being self-righteous toward one another. But both your ego and your wisdom are always accessible. My advice to you is that when people are adversarial, let them be that way and watch them stumble over their own egos. Don't get caught up or let anything or anyone shut off your heart from the well of your loving. Ultimately, everyone wants this, but not everyone knows how to get there. It's worth everything to live in that true place, anchored in a healthy and balanced sense of self.

SUGGESTIONS FOR THIS WEEK

1. Remember a time when you clashed with another person's ego. Write it down. Replay the situation. Now, go outside the situation, like an omniscient observer, and see if you can see the situation from the other person's point of view; put yourself in his shoes. Now, forgive yourself for any judgments you placed on yourself, the other person, and the situation. Come into a sense of peace and balance. Ask for your higher wisdom to preside over and guide you, so you can move forward. If ever this conflict should come up again, ask your higher wisdom to help you work in cooperation with the other person and find the "golden mean"—the middle ground.

2. When you are about to try something new in your life and you feel unsettled or outside of your comfort zone because you doubt yourself, counsel your ego and boost it up. Be self-supportive and say, "I have it in me to do this. I have the strength and ability to execute this new possibility." So move forward stepping into your strength with confidence. It may feel awkward at first, but keep practicing. You are doing it for you and for no one else. Your ego will be grateful it's been boosted. If you can't move forward on your own, find a friend who supports and encourages you. That's what friends are for!

3. Choose a character from history, a movie, literature, or a play. Seeing this character through the lens of inflated or deflated ego will make you aware of how ego plays a role in relationships and in life. For example, in the movie *Joy* with Jennifer Lawrence, Joy has such a strong ego that despite all of the rejection and obstacles blocking her path, her perseverance helps her rise above them and eventually helps her become

one of the most successful product developers in the country! Another example is Erin Brockovich, famously portrayed by Julia Roberts, who used her ego to mobilize others and defeat a corporation despite all the odds. Know how powerful it can be to educate and partner with your ego because it will help you withstand all obstacles.

18.

KNOW YOUR EXIT TIME

Fear is the cheapest room in the house. I would like to see you living in better conditions.

—Hafiz

When I was studying at RADA in London, one of my teachers told a story that has stayed with me throughout the years. Sir Ralph Richardson, a well-known and reputable actor who was a contemporary of Sir Laurence Olivier, was interviewed on television and asked, "What's one of your most memorable moments at the beginning of your career?" He described the following: He was hired for a small role in a play whose director was inconsistent about the directions he was giving to the actors, always changing his mind and confusing things. He had instructed Richardson to say one of his lines and exit stage right. The next day, the director instructed the actor to say his line and exit stage left. When he did that, the director reprimanded him for following the new direction. This happened quite a few times.

One day, the director told Richardson to say the line and exit stage right, not stage left as instructed the day before. In Richardson's own words, "I proceeded to exit stage right, to my dressing room to gather my things and then all the way home. I sent a note to him saying, 'I took my exit cue exactly as you directed and it led me all the way home. I will not be returning. Wishing you a wonderful production. Sincerely, Ralph Richardson.'"

I love this story. It made an impact on me as a young girl and actress. So often, I've felt that you have to put up with however people treat you. You've probably felt the same way—that you don't have the right to ask for something better. You feel so grateful for an opportunity that you accept bad treatment. You rationalize it by thinking, "I'm new to the job, I need to pay my dues" or "If I leave, there won't be anything else." You're acting from a space of scarcity.

If you remember my experience with a tyrannical director in the previous chapter, I knew that I had a choice and could leave, but I didn't because I really wanted the part. So I chose to stay and put up with her. But I did have a choice. You always have a choice. You don't have to be a victim. The trick is to listen for your exit cue.

I had to learn to know my exit time with a friend. Have you ever felt like you were moving apart from a friend, but you didn't know how to end it? Boyfriends are easier—there's a script for breaking up with them. But how do you break up with a "friend-friend"? When I moved back to Los Angeles to write my second book, after being in New York for eight years on my own, I re-kindled an old friendship with a woman who was in an emotionally turbulent marriage. We started supporting each other; she had marital challenges, I was building a new life. She was my buddy: we would work out together, chat daily, cheer each other on. But every other week, there was always an explosion in her relationship and a litany of problems I would listen to. We'd discuss the same problem, the same issues, over and over again, without any resolution. I was trying to be a good friend, but every time she would call and say, "Can we talk for a minute? I want to share with you what just happened," I would start to feel resentful. It was taking energy away from writing my book, making me unable to focus on creating.

I knew that I couldn't listen to the saga anymore and all the negative feelings around it. I finally found the strength to say to her, "Sweetheart, I really cannot listen to this issue with your husband anymore. I know it's a big part of your life because you have no intention of leaving him, or really doing anything about it. I just can't be a part of it anymore. I love you, but I need to take a break. I will send you my good thoughts, pray for you, but I need to focus on completing this book." And I meant it—in my heart I wished her the best.

She was hurt, of course. It was hard for me too. I was scared I'd hurt my friend, and I missed her, too. But I needed to embrace my book; she needed the dignity of her process in her relationship. Letting go of that friendship freed up space in me that I filled with creativity and other, positive relationships. Ultimately, I knew that my wisdom had guided me to this decision. It all worked out. I let go of my judgments. I felt grateful that I had found and followed my exit cue.

It is so hard to admit when a relationship—with a friend, romantic partner, or work colleague—has expired, but you can feel when a connection is draining you, making you feel resentful and frustrated. Fear will surface, fear of unknown consequences, fear that you'll blow your only shot at love, friendship, a job. I watched my mother move on when she had enough of my father's infidelities, temper outbursts, and erratic way of living. One day she herself burst out and said, "I'm taking my children and moving on." It was excruciating for her. In Athens, at this time, women didn't leave. They endured. She had no vocation of her own and relied on whatever my father provided as well as the "good graces" of her brothers. But move on she did! It was very challenging for her, for him, for me and my sister. As painful as it was, my mother knew her exit time had come.

It was all worth it in the end—the energy she directed toward that negative relationship, hoping and wondering if my father would ever change, was able to go into her own health and happiness and that of her children. It took great courage and trust for my mother to do what she did. I've seen so many women stay in loveless marriages because of the fear of being alone, social consequences, or financial instability, or for the children. They pay a great price; it takes a toll on their heart and being.

Putting yourself through the discomfort of change is certainly not easy. Leaving is hard, yes—you'll feel needy, disoriented, insecure, weird—but it's also empowering. It makes space for magnificent things. Just think, what if the breaking down of something that doesn't work is actually a breakthrough to something new and exciting?

As in a play, there are exit cues in life, and there is always another scene. The play doesn't stop. It just keeps building and unfolding. If you delay your exit time, the next scene can't begin. Trust yourself when you feel the *call* to exit. Don't be afraid of endings, because they empty the stage for something new to make its entrance.

SUGGESTIONS FOR THIS WEEK

1. Take an inventory of the relationships in your life. Be honest with yourself. It could be a professional, romantic, familial, medical, or social relationship. Write down if there's someone

or something in your life that you need to move on from. Ask for inner help and guidance. Daring to own your truth can bring you a surge of new energy.

2. Once you've identified that someone or something, write down in your journal what moving on would feel like for you. If there is a concern, a fear, talk it out with yourself or someone you trust whose wise support you value. When you decide to move on, give yourself a timeline. Slowly start to extricate yourself—at least you're facing the fact that it's time to exit. Support yourself in the process.

3. Write down your ideal new scene, with all the positive aspects of what it will feel like when you move on—give yourself latitude to use your creative imagination to its fullest. Just go there! Start imagining how you will feel with this new space and openness in your life, surrounded by love and support. Acting as if you already have what you want is a powerful tool to start manifesting it. Make it as real as possible, as if you have it right now.

19.

THE ART OF LETTING GO

Observe your own body. It breathes. You breathe when you are asleep, when you are no longer conscious of your own ideas of self-identity. Who, then, is breathing?

—Ilchi Lee

The day I was performing my hour-long one-woman show for PBS, *Conversations with the Goddesses*, filming outdoors in L.A. in front of two hundred people, I woke up extremely nervous. This was not a dress rehearsal but a live performance videotaped by four cameras in front of a large audience on a set designed to look like a luscious garden of the goddesses. As you probably have experienced, the first thing that goes when you're anxious is your breath. Your breath becomes tight, and your inhalations and exhalations become shorter.

One of my best friends, who teaches breathing coordination in New York, flew to L.A. to help me become centered through my breath so that I could perform from a place of relaxation. When I was on her massage table attempting to relax my jaw, diaphragm, and shoulders while trying to release my breath, she said the magic words "Darling, let yourself be breathed."

At that moment, an extraordinary thing happened. I let go.

Just like that. The part of me that was holding so tight—my anxiety about the outcome of the performance—loosened. I immediately understood that there was nothing I needed to do but let myself "be breathed" and let my breath flow in and out. I was completely aligned with my breath without actually thinking about my breath. I was overcome with an incredible sense of peace. Through relaxing my breath, I had made space for my spirit to come in. Something larger lives in us that is hidden in our breath. As Rumi says, "There is a way of breathing that's a shame and a suffocation, and there is another way of expiring, a love breath, that lets you open infinitely."

Once I arrived at the set, I kept moving from one thing to the next with the sense of riding this wave of being breathed. Everything had opened and relaxed. As the audience arrived and we were ready to shoot, I managed to stay on the wave that was carrying me. I felt joy and anticipation, but I was also very calm. As I began to perform, I sensed that the audience, the crew, and myself were all in sync with a collective calmness. A beautiful thing was happening. Everyone's spirit was coming into harmony. That presence remained until the end of the performance. As John Coltrane says, "God breathes through us so completely . . . so gently we hardly feel it . . . yet it is our everything."

What happened that day was a real transformational moment of learning of how to let go. I learned that I can always create distance between myself and what I'm going through. When we access that deeper part of ourselves that is connected to our breath, we start to surrender to something bigger that is breathing through us, which is the breath of life freely given to us. That breath is actually the pathway to love.

We have been conditioned with a fight-or-flight response—we are always thinking of things we need to do next. But by practicing slowing down the breath, you give a strong message to the brain that there is no danger and you are okay. There is no anxiety in the breath, unless you put it there. If you put worry into your breath, the breath becomes shallow and tight, and then you start to feel anxious and overwhelmed.

Start observing yourself while you go through your day. If you're rushing from one thing to another, take slow and deep breaths, which will help you be calmer and relaxed in all you have to accomplish.

Like everything else, this takes practice, like building a new muscle. You can practice anywhere: while you're walking, shopping, in a meeting, on the bus, in front of your computer doing your e-mails—you will start to carve new pathways inside of you and create a new sense of connection and calmness.

When I remember to practice this powerful gift that is embedded in my own breath, and I choose to turn my focus to it, I experience a freedom that is indescribable. Our emotions and our thoughts bind us. Our breath liberates us. So if we can get back to the power of the breath, we can live free.

GUIDED MEDITATION

Take a deep breath and relax. Take another deep breath, relax into your heart, and allow yourself to have some uninterrupted time. As you take your next breath, breathe in a deeper sense of letting go and as you exhale, let go of the tensions, the worries, the places inside of you where you are tight, and exhale with a sound . . . HHHHAAAA. As you take your next breath, observe the rising and falling of your breath, and ask yourself, "Who is breathing me?"

Take your right fist and clench it. Neutrally observe your right fist being clenched. There is your fist that you are clenching, and there is a part of you that is observing this clenched fist. That's the observer in you. Open your hand and release your fist. Do the same thing with your left hand: clench, observe, and release.

Scan your consciousness for areas in your life that feel like a clenched fist. When you get anxious, pressured, like you're missing out or not being at home with yourself, where in your body do you hold that tightness? Go there. Observe it. Breathe into it and start to release it as you exhale. Observe yourself experiencing all of these feelings. If you are sad, observe yourself feeling sad. No judgments. The same if you're feeling anxious, guilty, angry, or lonely. No judgments. Keep bringing your breath into all of these feelings. If you have fear about what will happen next, how are you going to meet your financial obligations, fears about your children, your parents, observe that feeling and let it go. No judgments. Keep observing yourself in the different aspects of your life, the thoughts and emotions that run through your mind and heart. Let the observer in you be awake. It's a sense of expansion. It's okay to have all of these feelings and thoughts, but you are so much more than that. As you observe the situations in your life, start to see the possibilities of freedom, happiness, relaxation, trust, calmness, joy, and a sense of oneness with yourself. Start to experience an awareness of being at home with yourself.

Let the larger part of you that is breathing you, your life force, breathe you deeply and fill your lungs, your brain, and your heart with the gratitude of your breath. Stay there for a few moments. Isn't it wonderful to be able to breathe freely? As Kabir says, "Tell me, what is God? He is the breath inside the breath."

When you're ready, gently open your eyes, wriggle your fingers, wriggle your toes, stretch your neck all around, take a sip of water so you can really ground yourself, and look around you with a new sense of what life would be like if you just became the observer of your life. Start to feel a sense of happiness inside, letting the observer reveal to you the possibilities of your life. Smile inside and outside. Inhale and as you exhale think, "Life is wonderful just because it is." Let yourself have this sense of optimism about your life, remembering that you have access to the freedom that comes with your breath and observation.

20.

CHECKING IN AND FOLLOWING UP

When I ask people what they want to experience most in their life, they often say, "I would like to feel safe in the world." I find that deep feeling of safety comes from trusting yourself. You can only trust yourself if you learn to listen to your own guidance and then follow through with what it tells you to do. You have to earn your own trust.

I believe we each have an inner compass that knows the direction of our lives at every second. When you are in tune with your compass, the guidance and wisdom that's inside of you becomes second nature. But you have to give yourself permission to listen to it.

Let me tell you a story about what happens when you ignore your inner guidance. I attended a conference where I spoke, signed books, and connected with many people. When I finished, a girlfriend of mine suggested we go shoe shopping together. My inner guidance steered me toward home; I was tired and just wanted to rest. But my friend's a delight to shop with, and I needed to get some comfortable shoes anyway. So I went out shopping. I bought a lovely pair of flats, and on my way out of the store, while looking on my phone for the Uber app, I didn't notice the curb. In a flash, I fell flat on my face, my handbag and new pair of shoes went into the street, and I sprained my ankle. I started to cry. My girlfriend and everyone around were so sweet and helped me to the waiting car.

What a lesson, though. I bypassed my inner guidance. Now my body will remember the fall, the pain, and the sprain the next time I'm tired but try to push it. No matter how basic the choice may seem—the choice between going out with a friend and staying home—you need to listen to that inner voice. Every day we are given hundreds of chances to listen to that voice.

We all do things we don't really want to do. We get swept up by the fear of missing out or displeasing others. We RSVP to events and dinners months in advance, before we have any way to know how we'll be feeling that day. And then we just end up resentful. Give yourself permission to not rush into deciding to do something or responding to someone. Take a few minutes, pause, and consider if this is something that you want to participate in, whatever it is: events with friends, more responsibilities at work, philanthropic causes, significant other's commitments, and so forth. To honor yourself, you need to build some really strong boundaries. Life is so much more joyful when you do things that you're fully engaged in.

It can be hard to hear that inner voice when there are all those other voices saying what you *should* be doing in your relationship, at work, with your money, with your life. Your "inner GPS" doesn't shout, it's more like a whisper, but it gives us directions and we have to attune ourselves so we can hear what it has to say. Learning to listen to this inner voice, through many situations in my life, has been a profound experience. Especially when it comes to taking care of myself and not overcommitting. It's especially hard when someone is asking for help and it pulls on your heartstrings. Even then, give yourself breathing space before saying yes and committing to something. Say, "Let me sleep on it" or "Can we circle back in a few days to check my schedule?" before jumping to yes. Make sure you're secure in your yes.

Let's say a group of your friends plans a dinner months in advance, when all of your calendars are free, and your intuition tells you that it may not work for you at that time. You have a choice to say "I'm not sure right now about my schedule, let's pencil it in and I'll let you know closer to that time." Give yourself space before committing to another thing that you might have to cancel. It is exercising your wisdom to look ahead and be honest with yourself. None of us wants to disappoint people by changing plans or canceling appointments we've made, but we often walk a thin line in being truthful about where we're at in the moment. Know that the most important loyalty is being true to ourselves. That's where the trust comes in and the sense of confidence begins to build.

This has a ripple effect on everything else we do. It builds self-esteem and a trust in ourselves that we're going to take care of ourselves and makes us less hectic, more at peace and centered. We are more clear about what is for us, and what is not for us. I now practice this awareness on a daily basis and take time to recalibrate about the little things in my life, as well as the big things. I often ask myself basic questions like "How do you feel about this commitment? What can I do to support you in that?" If situations occur where I have bypassed my inner knowing, I teach myself to say, "Okay, I'll remember that for next time. I didn't really honor what I heard." When we do this, we give the universe permission and say that we're open to receive what's available to us, and the abundance that is available to us can flow. We are no longer discounting ourselves, operating from the "right rules," from a sense of lack or scarcity, and overriding our inner knowing. Instead, we are permitting ourselves to value ourselves, our wisdom, and ultimately our true self.

GUIDED MEDITATION

This is a guided meditation to help you have greater attunement with yourself. So often our inner guidance is telling us things about our lives, about opportunities that we could take, how to respond to situations, what we need to do to recharge ourselves, how to say no, how to say yes, and when to say nothing.

But we often ignore it because we feel we have to please people, and because we feel we don't have a right to our own ways of being and doing we violate our inner guidance. So in this guided meditation, I want to show you how to honor your inner guidance.

Pick an area in your life where you are indecisive about what to do: you don't know what your next action should be, or maybe you are asked to do something and you aren't sure if you want to or not. Maybe it has to do with a relationship, and you need more clarity, more assistance. Imagine a beautiful yellow light filling you and surrounding you, making you alert and clear so you become a clean slate. Let this light now illuminate your path and your way, and ask yourself for a specific guidance in this area that you aren't clear about.

Ask yourself to be shown what it is that you need to do about that person or situation, or about the next action. Is there someone you need to reach out to? Do you need to be shown the truth of someone's character? Just listen for a moment. Check in with yourself—sometimes it is through an image, through a clear direction. Start to become aware of your inner guidance leading you, telling you, instructing you. We always know when we give ourselves permission to access our wiser part. If there is a decision that you've been sitting on, now you see what it is that you need to do. You are so grateful to have created the inner space to know and to see, and to know that you are never alone. You can actually take a few moments wherever you are to attune yourself to this inner guidance. When you are ready, open your eyes, and take your journal and your pen and write down what it is that you heard and saw. Was it an action you should take? Was it someone you should reach out to? Let yourself reveal your answers.

21.

MANAGING YOUR ENERGY

Whatever excites you, go do it. Whatever drains you, stop doing it.

—Derek Sivers

Every day, hundreds of things happen. From our personal lives to what's going on in the world to what's going on with people we interact with, there are endless things that pull us in many directions. No wonder we all feel stressed out! Plus there's the pressure to find a work–life balance, to be happy, and to live in a way that fulfills us.

Like all of us, I often start my day with a lot of external input: e-mails, deadlines, to-do lists. We all want to move from one thing to the next without feeling stressed, tired, and overwhelmed. I have found that managing my energy has a lot to do with staying connected to myself. Finding that place inside of me that is centered, steady, and calm is essential so I can navigate what's coming my way—including the energies I absorb from other people's emotional states. I've needed to learn to distinguish between what is mine and what belongs to other people. That has been a critical component to having a good day.

You are your first priority. Remembering that is a fundamental key to being balanced. When you find yourself feeling overwhelmed and bombarded by the countless things that come your way—especially with today's technology—your whole system becomes overloaded. You can lose clarity, your decision making can be clouded, your emotions can flood you, and you can start to feel caught in a tornado. Learning to back away from any environment that puts you into a tailspin is imperative.

I used to keep going no matter what. Even if I was overwhelmed, depleted, or pressured, I would just keep going. I thought that if I completed more tasks, I would feel better. Not true at all! Pressing the pause button at moments of tension is much more useful. Whether it's taking a walk, listening to uplifting music, telling a friend how I feel, doing jumping jacks, or whatever it takes to disconnect from the franticness, these breaks let me return renewed to my life.

What returns you to yourself? For me, the more grounded I am in my connection to myself, the more solid I feel in dealing with the outside world. A daily practice, whether it's meditation, prayer, contemplation, exercising, or self-care, builds an inner commitment to yourself that can help you stay steady. This radical self-care becomes a buffer against the world. With healthy boundaries, you'll protect yourself from taking in more than you can handle. I find that I can reconnect to myself if I ask myself, "What is the most loving and effective thing I can do for myself right now?" Sometimes, the answer is "Get off your smartphone, girl! Turn it off for a few minutes. Change your focus to something uplifting and creative. Take a moment to see the beauty around you. Stand up and stretch. Slow down your breath. Drink some water. Have a cup of tea. Go for a walk. Change your focus!"

Have you ever gone to a meeting or event feeling good but sometime over the course of the event started to feel off? It happens to me. When I begin to feel off, I know I have allowed something to take me off my center. Having the awareness to ask, "What/who is pulling me right now?" is a very empowering way to make yourself present again.

My mother faced so many challenges in her life. Throughout it all, she would take time out, have a cup of tea with her favorite digestive biscuits, and say, "There's nothing to do right now but enjoy my tea. I'm just going to let it marinate." Miraculously, assistance and solutions would show up. She was willing to get off the treadmill, not worry or overthink it, and allow grace to unfold. I watched her do this over and over again. She had total trust that the divine plan would always guide her. This surrender is the most loving and compassionate thing you can do for yourself: release the inner pressure, allow the shift to happen, and let yourself see the solution.

QUESTIONS TO ASK YOURSELF WHEN YOU FIND YOURSELF SPINNING

Start making a list. Answer these questions that will give you insights into your process:

➻ What is your foundation for maintaining a balanced energy?

➻ What are the nonnegotiable things you must do every day to remain centered and balanced?

➻ Start distinguishing what feelings or thoughts are yours and what are other people's.

→ What would healthy boundaries look and feel like between you, your environment, and other people?

→ How do you fill your tank daily and what are your ways of doing that?

By the end of the day, if you have lost yourself, reconnect back before you go to sleep and be grateful for all the little things that happen. End your day with gratitude, and it will return you back to you.

GUIDED MEDITATION

It's best to do this short guided meditation before you start your day.

Find a comfortable position and relax, letting go of any tensions and worries, and come into the presence of your heart. Take a deep breath and exhale with a sound, "Ahh." Slowing down your breath, observing the rise and fall of your breath. Stay centered in your heart. From this still place, start to set the intention of how you want your day to go, and how you want to maximize your energy and time as you engage with your work, people, and other tasks. Start to experience how you want to feel throughout the day. What do you need to do to take very good care of yourself? Make sure that you drink enough water, eat nutritious foods, take time to stretch, keep yourself relaxed when things get tense, and most of all, allow yourself to return to the power of your breath, keeping your breath open and relaxed. Start to see any areas where you might feel challenged today—maybe with deadlines, the beginning of new projects, meetings, and things you have to do in your personal life.

Start to set the intention that it's going to be a good and positive day, noticing how you stay centered, contained in your own energy, aligned with your truth, and bring joy into your day. Listen to your inner guidance, listen to when you start pressuring or demanding from yourself, and stay in a positive and loving place with yourself no matter what. Ask yourself to be aware of where you might be overextending, where you might need to ask for more support and give yourself permission to ask for what it is you want for your day. Ask from yourself, ask from others, and ask from the universal energy that is available to you. Fill yourself with light—any color that makes you feel vibrant and alive. Send a wave of light ahead of you to your day, to all your meetings, your interactions, your loved ones, even the people you may be having a challenging time with—send them positive waves of light and energy. See yourself staying centered throughout the day. See yourself returning to your center when you lose your balance. Promise yourself that today will be a day where you will move into greater acceptance of yourself, of others, and of your circumstances. You will use your creativity to master situations that may need solutions, resolutions, and completion. Envision giving yourself little moments to pause throughout the day and never rushing from one thing to the next. Recharge with moments of conscious breathing where you slow down your breath and fill your lungs and whole body with oxygen. Most of all, stay elevated, as clear as you can, always asking for the light to be with you, renewing you, energizing you, and nurturing you. Knowing that you have all the resources you need to make this a happy day.

See yourself taking time between your work mode and your rest mode at the end of the day, doing things that disconnect you from the world and connecting back to your source within. Even if it's only for a few moments. Always go to sleep with a sense of gratitude, giving thanks for yourself, for your life, for all the things you did, appreciating yourself and those around you, filling yourself with gratitude. When you're ready, now, take a deep breath and exhale with a sound, "Ahh." Stretch your neck left and right, shake your shoulders, extend your arms to open your energy field, and when you're ready, open your eyes, and you're ready to start your day having set a good intention of being centered, aligned, and happy. Know that this is going to be a wonderful day that you've created for yourself.

22

TRUE GLAMOUR

Beauty is not in the face; beauty is a light in the heart.

—Kahlil Gibran

After I completed my training as an actor in London, I moved to Hollywood to pursue my career. I was no longer in a world where "craft" was key, but in one where looks and appearances determine your success. I got wrapped up in the world of glamour, appearances, and "who's who." I got caught up in images and tried to imitate others' looks. (That was a period in my life when I prioritized my spiritual quest and really didn't care about what I wore or looked like—wearing long muumuus too often, complete with platform shoes.)

While I eventually found a balance, presenting myself well without letting it rule my life, I remember when I was always longing for a sense of being at home in my own body, regardless of my appearance and the attention I received. Making peace with this has freed me from depleting my energy seeking approval from others, trying to fit in. Years after my struggles in Hollywood, I relearned this message at an event in New York.

My sister invited me to the Glamour Awards at Carnegie Hall, an event at which awards are given to women who have made a difference in the world. She was presenting the award to Queen Rania of Jordan. True to its name, the event is very glamorous and everyone dresses their glamorous best. There's a red carpet, tons of photographers, celebrities, the whole nine yards.

Of course I had a gorgeous dress chosen for the evening, with accessories picked out. In preparation for the event, I had my hair done; I was going to stop back at home after my hair appointment to change into my perfect dress, but my hair took much longer than I expected (doesn't it always?). So I called my sister and said, "I have to go home, change, and meet you at Carnegie Hall." She said, "Darling, you don't have time to go all the way downtown. Get ready, and come back uptown before the event starts." She was right, I didn't have time.

I had a moment of complete panic. I was wearing a simple blue dress, a business jacket, and my short high heels. Nothing glam about it, but it would have to do. My wonderful hairdresser volunteered to help, offering to have the makeup artist at the salon retouch my makeup. I gratefully accepted. She then took a pair of fun earrings from her purse and said, "Here, wear these. You are great and your hair looks amazing, so nothing else matters. Just be you!"

Sitting in the cab, adjusting to the idea of what I was wearing versus what I had intended to wear, I decided to feel good about being myself despite what I was wearing. I couldn't put on my glam dress, so I decided to put on my glam aura.

I arrived on time and started talking with other attendees—fascinating people, celebrities, award winners—not feeling self-conscious or judging what I was wearing. There I was being photographed with the likes of Cher, Jennifer Aniston, and Fergie from the Black Eyed Peas, her one-shoulder red dress slit up the side with a train in the back, and her long blond hair styled like that of a 1920s movie star. The embodiment of glam. But even next to her I felt totally lit up and at home with myself!

What a lesson. I realized that what I wear has nothing to do with who I am and how I feel about myself. Sitting in the audience at Carnegie Hall, I felt such gratitude for these amazing women and the good work they've done in the world. My heart was swelling with the goodness of humanity.

That feeling carried me throughout the evening, and it was so much bigger than my dress. When interacting with other attendees, instead of focusing on the fashion, celebrity, and glamour of the event, I was focused on appreciating and connecting with others in an authentic way. This evening shifted my focus from external validation to internal acceptance.

A young friend of mine who worked as a model really took this lesson to heart. She became quite well known, traveling throughout Europe with top designers—the epitome of glamour. One day, she took part in a goodwill project for a nonprofit devoted to building schools in Africa. There she was, a supermodel accustomed to haute couture, surrounded by people who wore the same outfit day after day, and many didn't have shoes. What a contrast. It so profoundly impacted her that she left the modeling world and a life of excess, and committed herself to the mission of this nonprofit.

Don't get me wrong. I still have my feminine vanity and want to look good when I see people or when I have a speaking engagement. But I learned to recognize that the energy and intention I invest in my outer appearance needs to be in proportion to its worth—and no amount of glitz can outshine your inner light. Think about the best wedding you've ever been to—was it the expensive, over-the-top wedding, or the one where you could really kick up your heels and celebrate with your loved ones?

We're all programmed to get lost in the illusion of glamour. It's extremely seductive. If you're not careful and aware, you can feel like you never measure up and eventually lose yourself in that lie. If you get caught in the glamour trap, thinking that it's something you don't have but others do, you are doing yourself a disservice. The truth of it is, underneath, we are all just people.

Who you are, what you can radiate, the warmth of your being can outshine the Hope Diamond. Once you have that light lit, go ahead and put on a lovely outfit with fabulous shoes and get your hair and makeup done, whatever it is that enhances the beauty inside—your true glamour.

Your essence and inner beauty will always draw people to you. No one will remember what you wore, but they will always remember how they felt in your presence.

GUIDED MEDITATION

This is a guided meditation to connect with your inner beauty. You can do this meditation when you are about to go to a function, event, meeting, date, or any time you might need some additional self-confidence. You can open up your energy field—the energy that surrounds your body—by pointing your pointer finger and middle finger on each hand toward your temples and very slowly extending your fingers outward, left hand going left and right hand going right, like you're pulling a string from your temples, until your arms are fully extended and your fingers are pointing away from you. Feel your energy extending to fill the space you are in, all the way from right to left.

Now place your two fingers on the top of your head and

imagine your energy extending all the way up to the ceiling. Now imagine that there's an energy extending from the bottom of your feet, grounding you all the way down to the floor. This should make you feel way bigger in your energy, encompassing the whole room. Connect with your heart and take a deep breath, and you will probably feel like your body is in this energy field. Your body might feel a little smaller, and your energy field way bigger. Now place colors in this energy field around you. It will make your aura—the energy around your body—very vital and bright. Let's imagine a beautiful yellow color energizing you; a beautiful blue giving you a brightness and a joy; a lovely pink making you feel beautiful, sweet, and calm. Now imagine a golden light swirling around you, keep putting layers and layers of golden light around you. Inside out, you start to experience this golden light, this golden presence, and it fills you and you start to feel so beautiful. Lit up from the inside, out. It's a beauty that is beyond your physical attributes. It is a beauty of your presence. You start to fill your heart with gratitude, knowing that you are way more than your physical attributes and looks. There is an inner glow that comes from within, a joy of who you are. Allow yourself to breathe that in and see yourself smiling because you are discovering the secret of your inner beauty.

Now take a moment to imagine yourself attending the function, and expand your energy, glowing from the inside out. Not comparing yourself at all to anyone, not caring about what anyone thinks of you. But steady, strong, and confident in your own energy. Knowing there's an inner light that sustains you and that you have access to at any time. Fill yourself with that energy, see yourself being with it, interacting with it, while you stay present in your presence.

Know that at any moment you might feel your energy is lowering itself, you can access this visualization. Take your hands and place them on top of your heart, and know that this energy is anchored right there in your heart. Tell yourself, "I am beautiful. I am confident. I radiate from the inside out." You feel warm, you feel vibrant, and you feel secure. When you are ready, you can open your eyes, and you're ready to do whatever you have to do and go wherever you have to go, full of the beauty of you.

23.

MONEY, MONEY, MONEY!

When I chased after money, I never had enough. When I got my life on purpose and focused on giving of myself and everything that arrived into my life, then I was prosperous.

—Wayne Dyer

Money issues are usually not about money. They are often about something deeper, something inside us that needs to be resolved—an inner conflict, a sense of entitlement, or a feeling of lack and fear that we just won't have enough. I'm not here to tell you how to invest or manage your money. I'll leave that to other experts. I want to shed light on your beliefs, attitudes, and consciousness about money and assist you in getting as free as possible from your self-limiting beliefs about it. Money is a teacher—a reflection and a symbol of the way we see ourselves as worthy or unworthy, and a reminder that we often carry old wounds around the topic of money. Or perhaps we are reliving our parents' story.

At a women's group that I attended recently, the presenter asked, "How many of you fear that you will end up being a bag lady?" I was absolutely surprised to see the majority of these successful working women raised their hands! Everyone in the room had the fear that everything could be taken away from them at any time and they would end up in the street. This was such a shock to me, since it's the opposite of how I've felt all my life. I'm not saying I was born with a silver spoon in my mouth. But I've always thought that I would have enough and be okay no matter how much money I had in my bank account.

I think this belief came from my mother, who was a naturally generous person regardless of what she had or didn't have. People responded to her generosity and gave back to her. She had a fundamental trust that life would always support her. She kept this attitude even when she separated from my father and had only a small allowance that rarely covered our expenses and didn't come close to paying for the way she wanted to raise us.

I realized much later in my life that the fundamental trust my mom radiated and communicated to us was rooted in a sense of abundance. When my parents were still together, my father would often call at the last minute to let my mom know that he was bringing guests home for dinner. Unruffled, my mom would look in the kitchen. Instead of saying there wasn't enough food, she would fashion a feast from whatever we had. It was like the parable of feeding the multitude with just a few fish and a loaf of bread. She always found a way to make enough food for our guests. At other times, when money was scarce, she would spend it on something special for my sister and me, so that *we never felt like we didn't have enough.* Her attitude of abundance kept us from comparing ourselves to people who had more than we did, and kept us from thinking that *we were of lesser value.* Everyone is conditioned to believe in the illusion that the people with the most money are somehow more worthy than others. My mother saw right through this cultural lie and wasn't about to let her daughters judge themselves or anyone else based on the size of a bank account.

When I was about nine years old, my father had a very rich friend who would pick him up every Sunday morning for the races. We had a modest suburban home, and my father's friend had a Jaguar with a chauffeur. I remember looking at this beautiful shiny car arriving for my father when my family didn't even have a car and traveled by bus, on foot, or with friends who had cars. I asked my mother a very innocent question, "Mummy, are we rich?" My mother, without missing a beat, sat me down and said, "We are very, very wealthy, which has nothing to do with money. Being wealthy has to do with being educated, sharing what you have, a thirst for knowledge, learning about the arts, knowing that you have love and friendships and gifts and talents that are unique to you. It's knowing you can study and develop your attributes so that you can go out into the world and serve other people and learn how to be joyful, happy, and have a meaningful life. This has nothing to do with money. You can have a lot of money and not have any of these things. If you want to go make money, you can go do that, too." I have never forgotten the power of my mother's fiercely passionate speech about wealth versus riches and the impact that it had on my young self.

In our society we attach so much worth, status, and power to how much money we have. Over the years, I have watched many wealthy, successful people guard and protect their money because they are in constant fear that they may lose it. I've also seen the opposite—people who have very little but live with an attitude of abundance and are always generous and engaged in the service of helping others. I've met others whose life goal is to make more money; it's their primary motivation. In the end, if there isn't anything underneath the motive and focus on money, people can feel empty and bereft. Relying on money to give us our sense of worth and purpose is hollow because all of the things that money can buy are temporary.

My father would self-sabotage his success, and when he would make money, he would have a hard time keeping it. When he made it, he spent it, often gambling, at the expense of his family. When he wasn't earning it, he was constantly worried about it and in fear of it. He was one of the millions who are locked in a primal, emotional battle with the concept of money, never at peace with it and never feeling worthy enough to build a life of financial stability. My mother, on the other hand, lived with that "attitude of gratitude" and expected everything to work out. Generosity flowed all around her, and everyone shared with her in the same way that she shared with them. I was caught in the middle of these two opposite relationships to money, and I had to find my footing and get comfortable within myself by recognizing this. I had to take time to heal my confusion about the role of money in my life. Many of us are influenced by deeply rooted issues around money that we are not conscious of, and yet they are controlling the way we handle money. Take the time to get to the root of your money attitude. You will be so glad that you did!

I struggled a lot to understand the energy of money and what I learned is that it's really about an *exchange of energy*. When I started to integrate spirituality and money, I realized that I had always looked at money as separate from my spiritual life. After all, money has such a bad rap—it's the "root of all evil"—so I thought that money couldn't possibly be spiritual. But the principle of tithing liberated my understanding of money. When I started tithing 10 percent of my earnings to my spiritual church, where I feel so connected, something started to open up inside me. As I tithed, I felt as though I was opening a space for more to come in. I was bringing a greater awareness into the money part of my life, so that money became completely integrated into my spirituality. It wasn't about the amount of money, but the intention behind my giving it. Once my intention was completely connected to spirit, and I started to spiritualize the money, I had this incredible feeling of affluence. I became hyperaware of the places in me that had tightened with fear about not having enough, fear of looking at how much I had in my bank account, or panic when I didn't know where the next paycheck was coming from. Something shifted. My body felt different when I tithed and relaxed my attitude about money. I didn't want to be preoccupied with money. Don't get me wrong, I love beautiful things. So I had to also open up and say, "I love *being paid* for what I do. But my *value* has nothing to do with money." *I wanted money to be in a natural flow in my life, just like everything else.* When I started to tithe, I gave it over and let go of the fear that I was "in lack."

Think about it. We have all received the check at a restaurant that was higher than what we expected it to be. Or panicked at our paycheck, realizing, "After I pay all my bills, there won't be anything left!" The next time this happens, pay attention to your body. Does it tighten up? Do you have that funny feeling in your stomach? Getting yourself healthy in your attitude toward money and surrendering to the graceful flow of giving and receiving helps to release the tension about money. This takes awareness and intentionality about living within your means and not having shame about where you're at when your friends may have more.

In London I was dating a composer who often had work but sometimes didn't. When he was worried about where his next paycheck was coming from, he would go buy a new silk tie to give himself the message that it was going to be okay, telling himself, "You're good at what you do, and work is coming." He didn't allow himself to go into fear or a sense of lack, and yet he didn't spend frivolously. He used his silk tie as a physical reminder to maintain his abundance consciousness and trust that the next job was around the corner.

Make your life about qualities and worthy values instead of things: generosity, joy, sharing yourself, faith, hope, trust, caring, loving, listening, learning, gratitude. Take total responsibility for your relationship to money. Respect it and don't worry every time you spend a dime. And, just as my friend did, love yourself enough and trust your relationship to money enough to get that silk tie (or whatever it is that you love), and allow yourself to trust in the generosity of the universe. Know that your source is infinite and your value is priceless.

SUGGESTIONS FOR THIS WEEK

1. Journal about your beliefs about money. Where do they come from? What did your parents teach you? How does this relate to your sense of self-worth? Be as specific as you can. For thirty-two days in a row (the time that psychologists think it takes to create a new pattern in the brain) try to be aware every time a fear, doubt, or concern about money comes up. Ask yourself what this is about and *do something that will help you open up*. Help someone else who has less than you. Be generous and shift the *contraction* about money. If you don't have a few extra dollars, give your time to help others. Cook a meal for friends. Anything that makes you feel generous and abundant. Whenever you feel this tightness, just do something to release it.

2. Consider finding a mentor who has a very healthy relationship with money, with whom you feel safe sharing and discussing your financial reality. This could include making a budget, saving for your short- and long-term vision, and learning how to spend responsibly and joyfully. Remember, it's not about the amount, it's about your relationship with money.

3. Choose your vehicle for giving. Find what makes you feel wealthy and don't make it about the money. Experiment! For you, this may be your favorite nonprofit or a cause that you respect because your values are in alignment with it. Find what makes you happy and let yourself open up to the joy of giving without the worry of not having enough. You are not your paycheck.

24.

THE SACRED PRIVILEGE OF PARENTHOOD

We do not believe in ourselves until someone reveals that deep inside us there is something valuable, worth listening to, worthy of our trust, sacred to our touch.

—e. e. cummings

Recently, at a dinner party, I asked the woman next to me, "What do you do?" She replied apologetically, "I'm just a stay-at-home mom." *Just?* Honestly, I can't think of anything more important in this world than being a parent! Raising a human being must never be taken lightly. You are raising the next generation. Give yourself a lot of credit and kindness in the huge responsibility you have undertaken. The more appreciative and compassionate you are with yourself, the more centered you will be to handle the challenges with your child.

Although I have never been a parent myself, I have had the privilege of seeing my two nieces grow up. During their teenage years, I coparented them with my sister and mother, all of us living together. My sister has a great expression: "You take the child out, and put the guilt in." Once you're a mom, you're constantly pulled by a powerful mothering instinct while also pulled to have a life and work of your own. This juggling exhausts most parents, especially in the first few years. Even tougher are the teenage years. Teenagers are simultaneously going through physical and emotional changes as they try to create their own identity. Hormones are racing through their bodies, and their brains are changing. They don't really know who they are. I'm sure all parents have thought, "Who are you?" as they observe their child trying to be his own person and move in the direction of becoming himself.

There are hundreds of books about parenthood, many of them valuable. I've watched friends and family raise their children, and here are the five most important principles for raising kids who are honest, expressive, happy, and healthy—while you foster your own well-being, too:

Rule 1: *Take care of yourself.* A great gift you can give a child is to be centered in your well-being. Children can't help feeling responsible for their parents' relationship issues and want to fix things when their parents aren't happy together. Children love happy parents. I know for myself that when I saw my parents being kind and loving with each other, I felt a big weight lifted off me. However, it is also such a relief for children when the fighting stops and unhappy parents separate. As wonderful and amazing as my mother was, I would have been happier to see her taking care of herself instead of denying herself a life of her own.

Rule 2: *Never ever compare your children to each other.* Each child comes with his or her own blueprint or nature. Learning to honor your children for who they are is vital and imperative. My sister was a brilliant A+ student. I loved art, music, dancing, and all forms of creativity. I found school challenging and would often pray for my math teacher to die! When we got our report cards, my mother surprised both of us with flowers, even if my sister had gotten an A and me a C. My mother was teaching me that I wasn't "less than" anyone. She didn't compare my math skills to my sister's, but instead reinforced and celebrated my unique gifts.

My mother was passionate about my sister and me going after our dreams. She always told us, "I don't care if you fail or succeed, I won't love you any less. I just want to see you pursuing the things you love to do." It took a lot of the pressure away to know that we didn't have to be successful to be loved and know that failure is part of success. Talk to your children about your own struggles. It allows them to understand failure as a stepping-stone to success.

Rule 3: *Praise your children.* Tell them as often as you can that they are valuable human beings who are worthy and lovable—and that you love them. Hug them, be tender and kind, and always allow quality time to listen to them. Validate your children for the great people they are. Create a safe space for them to tell you what's really going on with them, their friends, their world—with no judgment. When my sister and I came home from school, we sat for hours in the kitchen with our mom discussing our day—how it went, the challenges we were facing, the boys we liked, how the other girls acted toward us, and what we thought of our teachers. Do not criticize your children, but focus instead on supporting their strengths and the good they do.

Rule 4: *Give them ammunition to handle their challenges.* Don't leave them "hanging" with their struggles because this will create insecurity in the years to come. If your children need support with particular subjects, find mentors or tutors or older students who can speak their language and empower them to excel. My mother recognized my math deficiency and hired my math teacher to tutor me. This made me feel very supported and removed a lot of the angst I had surrounding this subject.

Rule 5: *Communicate . . . communicate . . . communicate!* It is so important for your child to understand and be aware of what's *really* going on at home. When my parents separated, my mom moved us into a new house after the summer holidays, without my dad. She didn't tell me that she and my dad were separating, so it came as a complete shock. My mom was too afraid or didn't know how to tell me, so I had to deal not only with the separation from my father but also with the hidden truth of what was happening in my family. I had to adjust without an explanation—a very hard thing to do when you are twelve years old. Tell your children what's going on (trust me, they already sense something's wrong) and make sure they understand it has nothing to do with them—that it's your issue, your problem.

As children grow up, they'll be faced with the big challenges of life—these might be anything from choosing a career, finding ways to express their gifts, to making a living, and some are faced with even greater challenges such as getting caught up in addiction or an eating disorder, experiencing depression or anxiety, dating a destructive boyfriend or girlfriend, or dealing with peer pressure. Seeing our children suffer is the most difficult part of being a parent. As a parent, you may need a lot of support handling these challenges. It's important that you maintain your wellbeing while you are trying to help your child. Share your struggles with your friends and ask them to support you; if they are suffering from emotional problems, read studies about the symptoms your child is experiencing, and find great doctors who don't overmedicate and will be willing to listen to your concerns and be there for you and your child; talk to other parents who are dealing with similar problems; and know that there are always solutions and support for you available and that you never have to face things alone. As a parent you may think that your child's struggles are your fault. Remember that each child is on his or her own path and takes on learning experiences in order to overcome personal challenges and grow stronger.

Our children become our greatest teachers in every way. They test our patience, our ability to love and to accept unconditionally, to learn new ways to be in the parent-child relationship, and they test our flexibility. They teach us from their innocent wisdom to see life through their eyes. Over and over again I have heard parents say, "I didn't know what love was like until I had my first child." Our children, more than anything, teach us to love unconditionally.

PRACTICES FOR BEING AUTHENTIC AND HONEST WITH YOUR CHILDREN

•▸ Write a letter to your children expressing what they mean to you and the ways in which their presence in your life has changed you. Frame the letter and give it to them as a reminder of how much you love them. Write them a letter as often as you feel like it, expressing your love and your joy seeing them grow.

- Have dates with your children. Create special outings and allow them to let their imagination flow freely, without censoring them. Talk about their future—the sky is the limit! Help them create vision boards for what they can become. Don't wait for birthdays, Christmas, or Valentine's Day. The best present you can give your child is *your time*.

- Work on your tendency to worry and trust that they're okay. When they don't call or text you, or don't keep you informed about their outings, trust that it's going to be okay. This helps them build their own independence. You can express to them how much you appreciate it when they communicate with you, but you can't force them to communicate or guilt-trip them into staying in touch. You don't want that kind of dynamic with your children!

- Always continue to work on your own happiness and growth by finding activities that keep you creative and engaged with new things. Prepare yourself for the time they will leave and go on to their own lives, maybe even in a different city or country. As they grow and move on, letting go is one of the biggest lessons in parenthood. Allow your children to find their own voice and their own tasks. The love between you will always be there— focus on that, it will always fill your heart.

25

DON'T RELINQUISH YOUR INNER AUTHORITY

Never abandon your inner wisdom because you think that others know better.

—Elli Stassinopoulos (my mom)

When we were young, my sister and I would ask for my mother's advice about different situations in our lives. My mother had a habit of not telling us what to do; in her relaxed, wise-owl way, she would say, "Darling, let it marinate. There's no rush. The answers will come." This forced us to trust ourselves and to know that we knew.

Now that we are adults, my sister often asks my advice on what she should do about situations; we discuss it and then I tell her my opinion. And then she does what she wants to do. We often laugh about it, and I give her a hard time the next time she asks for my opinion. But she says, "Running it by you helps me solidify the answer within myself."

So many of us make a habit of relinquishing our inner authority. It could be to a therapist, doctor, financial adviser, or salesperson—we surrender our inner knowing because they're the "experts." We also give over our authority to family, friends, significant others, or teachers because we value their opinion and we think they want what's best for us. But whatever advice comes your way, no matter from whom, check in with yourself. You know what happens when you disregard your inner guidance? You feel like you can't trust yourself and your inner knowing.

Too often we seek advice from other people, and, as you've probably noticed, people looove giving advice. A lot of the time people give their advice unsolicited, which can be very irritating. How many times have people had an opinion about anything from your diet, your relationships, your clothes, your hair, to how you manage your money or plan your vacations? You can easily fall into the trap of denying your own wisdom and following someone else's advice against your better judgment.

After I wrote my book *Conversations with the Goddesses*, I put together workshops called "Manifesting Golden Opportunities" to teach people how to create what they wanted in their lives. I asked the participants to converse with the different aspects of themselves and ask for insights with problems they were facing. One woman was having intimacy issues with her husband, so she asked Aphrodite what she could do about it. The Aphrodite inside her advised, "Don't wear socks in bed." Which made total sense to her! The big, thick socks she wore in bed turned her husband off. So she started wearing lingerie instead.

Another women conversed with her Hestia, goddess of the sacred, asking, "Why am I always feeling so tired?" Hestia replied, "You're allowing others to drain you." Right on for her! Another woman was dealing with a legal problem, and Athena, goddess of justice and wisdom, told her to find a new lawyer who was more savvy and sharper, someone who could protect her. All the answers were direct and specific because we had created a trusting, safe environment in which each person could listen to the answers that came from within.

There have been many times when I begin to quietly commune with my spirit, asking for guidance, but the next thing I know, my smartphone rings and then, after answering, I get caught up in other things—e-mails, texts, social media, news. The world seems to be set up this way. It takes a lot of vigilance to establish this new practice of creating a quiet time to listen to yourself. When you allow yourself uninterrupted time for inner guidance, the higher wisdom gives you solutions.

It's unfortunate that we as a society have lost the habit of taking precious time to reflect and turn inward for guidance, inspiration, and answers. We are so accustomed to be outwardly directed, constantly being connected to the outside world, so that when we turn inward we turn deaf and dumb. Tired of its competition with Google, our spirit shuts down. But the truth is, our all-knowing spirit is where we should go for answers. For this guidance to be present, we have to ask, and to make space for it.

A friend of mine lost most of her money from a failed business venture and a declining stock market; she couldn't pay her rent or medical bills. A very successful woman, she had a difficult time asking for help. She also has a very rich spiritual life. In communion with her spirit, she heard multiple times that she should ask for help from her estranged ex-husband. The spirit continued to nudge her for months. One day, she finally found the courage to call him. To her complete amazement, he said, without hesitation, "I would love to help you. I always felt like I owed you." She was stunned and speechless. He helped her financially until she was able to get back on her feet and support herself. She was humbled and said to me, "I will never again underestimate the mysterious way the spirit works through us and provides."

Make your spirit an ally. Converse with it regularly. Ask it questions and write down your answers. Keep a journal that is for you and your inner communion.

JOURNALING ACTIVITY

Turn on some quiet, meditative music and light a candle. Find a few moments in your day when you won't be interrupted. Beginning or end, doesn't matter. Think about a situation in your life where you feel stuck or could really use some inner guidance. Take your journal and at the top of a page, write the words "Spirit speaks to me." As you center in yourself, quieting your mind, take a pen and start writing what you hear inside—without censoring or second-guessing, just what spirit says to you. The answer might be short, even one word, or long, might not even make sense to you, just keep writing. Take as much time as you need, giving yourself permission to receive guidance without any judgments. When you finish, give thanks to your wisdom for speaking to you. Then go about your day and see if there is any specific answer given to you, anything you need to follow up on, and if there is, make sure you follow through to see if the direction you've been given makes a difference in your life.

26.

GET BEYOND COMPARISON

Comparison is the Thief of Joy.

—Theodore Roosevelt

My sister was always a brilliant A+ student. She loved math, economics and reading books. I was a free-spirited girl who wanted to dance, act, have a good time, and love people. I always wanted everyone to be happy. We were completely different, but my mother never compared us to each other. When I didn't do well in math class, she would say, "You weren't born to do math, but to use your own gifts." Despite this loving attitude, I would still think, "Maybe I should be achieving the way my sister does."

Then, to make matters worse, I became an actress. Of course, I compared myself to other actors and started to feel jealous, wondering why they were getting parts and I wasn't. I felt this for a long time. As I evolved and grew and learned about myself, I got to see how this kind of comparison is really a form of self-abuse. It robbed me of my own energy, my gifts, my light. It's a denial of your own life. But it's very much a part of human nature.

Comparison and jealousy can also serve a purpose. They tell

you that you don't yet know yourself. Because when you know your true self and are aligned with your own path, you no longer look left and right, and second-guess yourself. Don't judge your jealousy when it comes up; observe it and say, "That's interesting. My mind is thinking about this person and what she has." But then gently redirect your thoughts and affirm, "I am a cocreator of my life and what is it that I want to create for myself?" Give yourself permission to dig deeper and go create what you want.

Maybe you look at someone and think, "Gee, this person is getting a promotion and making more money than me, and we're the same age. What is he doing that's so different than me?" All that's different is that he has a promotion and a bigger paycheck. He is still a person with struggles and fears, and who knows what will happen tomorrow? Now, there's nothing wrong with observing someone like that as an example and inspiration to analyze what he's doing to excel and see what you can do better. I had to learn that lesson the hard way when I realized that I wasn't getting the parts I wanted, because I had a whole other purpose and calling waiting for me.

There were times when I so wanted the right relationship and romantic love. I would go to a party or event and see a couple expressing their affection, and I would feel like I was missing out. Until one day it dawned on me that a romantic relationship wasn't going to complete my life—that my path was different. Be wise when that voice of comparison comes to you, and don't give it credence; observe it and let it pass by like clouds. Take it as an opportunity to look at an area of your life where you haven't fully engaged or given your all. So use these feelings as an indicator that something needs to be addressed, that you need to start fully participating in your life.

The grass isn't always greener on the other side, because you never know what soil it's planted in. So don't make any assumptions about what you see because the truth is, we don't know what people are going through, what a relationship looks like on the inside, how many family gatherings a person had to miss to get the promotion, or how they feel when they go to bed at night. Be grateful for where you are.

Here's another way to think about it. Do you think Stevie Wonder was wondering what Bob Dylan was writing when he was composing, "I Just Called to Say I Love You"? Do you think Adele was comparing her voice to Celine Dion's the first time she belted out "Someone Like You"? Do you think a beautiful lemon tree is looking at a fig tree and thinking, "Oh man, I wish I weren't so sour"? No! They're all busy being themselves.

I wholeheartedly encourage you to figure out where your tendency for comparison comes from, without judgment, and see it for what it is: a lie. A distraction from your own path. Then, take your own energy back to yourself and put it 100 percent into your own life. Stand in your own power, magnificence, and destiny.

GUIDED MEDITATION

Find a comfortable position and relax as you allow the natural flow of your exhalation and inhalation. Focus on your heart and imagine a beautiful white light, filling you, surrounding you, and protecting you. Look at all the areas of your life: your health, work, relationships, emotional well-being, home environment, and see if you want them to be better, more balanced, or improved in any way. Look at the areas of your life where you tend to go outside yourself and look at someone else's life and think they have it so much better. Challenge that thought by telling yourself, "I really, in truth, don't know what anyone else is going through despite appearances." So wherever there are thoughts and emotions of comparisons with others, in any area, allow yourself to look at those thoughts and gently bring them back to you, to your heart, with a feeling of gratefulness for your life. Be truly grateful for who you are and what you have. Look at everything in your life as a blessing. If there is a particular area where you would like something to be different, start to visualize and see in your creative imagination what that would be like. What would you have to do, accept, and change in order for that area to be the way you would like it to be? Make a mental note of what's being told to you and listen. Listen from a place of acceptance, letting go of any judgment you may have about yourself and your life. Take a moment right now, in your quietness, to let go of the judgments, comparisons, any sense of lack, any sense of being or feeling less. In truth, you are perfect just the way you are, right now. Take a deep breath and exhale. Take another deep breath and relax into the sense of allowing yourself to know that you have all the resources and abilities to make your life the way you want it to be. Allow this inner light to shine on you, warm you, illuminate you. Do not look anywhere else but inside yourself; know your new direction, your next action steps; and with a sense of clarity and new beginnings, gently return to full awareness here and open your eyes. Exhale with a sound, "Ahh." Wriggle your fingers and toes. Shake your shoulders and let go of anything that's preoccupying you, and give thanks for this new awareness you have inside of you. It would be wonderful to jot down in your journal what you heard and saw, and what new direction was given to you. One small thing you take in the new direction of knowing that you are enough, and perfect just the way you are.

27

ENOUGH OF FEELING YOU'RE NOT ENOUGH

The one thing you can control is how you treat yourself. And that one thing can change everything.

—Leeana Tankersley

Everybody struggles with the feeling of not being enough. Some people have this feeling, but they override it, they don't give it too much credence, they keep going, they even use it as motivation to get ahead. Some people put it center stage, they give it a script and a story line, and put a spotlight on it. It has a starring role in their lives and it stops them from living their lives.

This belief has different disguises: financial, familial, relational, physical, educational. One of the ways it manifests is the game of hierarchy, the more important people versus the less important people. I was lucky enough to be raised in a home with a mother who didn't grovel to hierarchy; to her, people were people, all the same, equally important. She made sure that she reinforced in my sister and me the value of who we were, regardless of money or class or living in a one-bedroom apartment in Greece. There was always a sense that we were enough and we had enough because there was always enough love in our home.

However solid my upbringing was, the "not good enough" feeling started to surface in me at a later age when I traveled to England to study acting. At drama school in London, I was acknowledged for my talent despite being one of the youngest in my class. However, I had a "funny" Greek accent and didn't speak the "Queen's English." I felt different and like an outsider. I walked around feeling unsettled and insecure, which of course was natural since I was eighteen and from a different culture. This feeling stayed with me when I moved to Los Angeles, where I tried to make it as an actress but didn't succeed. I told myself that I was inadequate, rather than different and unique. I turned against myself, deciding that not fitting in meant I wasn't enough. Such an untruthful leap!

I found solace in my quest for spirit and dove into my inner work with a visceral fervor. At some point, I realized that I was much more than my dream of becoming a successful actress, finding the perfect relationship, and being recognized in the world. I started to separate from my worldly identity, and the walls to my inner being began to crumble. The girl I left behind in Greece was a beautiful, lovable, vulnerable, tender being—completely whole. She was lacking in nothing but experience, and she wasn't sure how to bring her essence into the world.

There was a moment when I experienced this shift from not feeling enough to loving and accepting myself right where I was. I was traveling with my spiritual teacher John-Roger in London. While sitting in a café enjoying coffee and pâtisseries and reading the London *Times*, I opened the theater page, and to my surprise I saw that one of my classmates from RADA was starring in a play on the West End. My immediate thought was "Wow. He's starring in a play and what have I been doing with my life?" As

I was sharing the news with my teacher, he read my mind: "Oh, he's starring on the West End and what have you been doing with your life?" I felt like the ground had fallen out from beneath my feet. My internal self-criticism was now in my face.

The whole afternoon I walked around feeling deflated and depleted, dragging myself all over London. That night at dinner, John-Roger turned to me, gave me a big heartfelt hug, and said, "You have been running that belief against yourself for a long time. So I had to do 'surgery' to bring it to the surface and get it out of you." I started to laugh and cry. I had been judging myself, comparing myself and coming up short, for quite some time, and this is not a fun way to live. It cuts off your circulation and self-love. I suddenly saw the irrationality in thinking this way. I was following my life's path, and my acting classmate was following his; one has nothing to do with the other. At that moment, I started moving toward self-acceptance and gratitude for my life. As I opened up to my own gifts and path, I started to experience the profound feeling of being enough.

The willingness to love and accept yourself, even if you don't know how, is the starting point to letting go of the judgment and comparison. It is the willingness to see and believe that you are enough no matter what. It is saying to yourself, I don't feel like I'm enough, but you know what? I am willing to open the windows and let the air come in. I can breathe "enoughness" into me. I am willing to see all of the possibilities. I am willing to let go of my comparisons and judgments. Spirit then meets us with unconditional love. And then we are able to access that fullness regardless of whether we have the right job, enough money, or a relationship we long for. Experiencing our fullness has nothing to do with what we have in the world. This fullness of self is our birthright.

When this epiphany hit me and I stepped into my "Agapi-ness," I started to be a proactive human being in the world, contributing from a place of "being more than enough." From that place, it was extraordinary how the world responded. Opportunities came to me: I was asked to write books, perform, conduct seminars, and speak at conferences, and people sought my guidance for their well-being. As I was helping make a difference in people's lives, I started to feel fulfilled. Life was happening from the inside out. When you recognize that you are more than enough, you are filled with the richness of you and can tap into the joy of your life as it is.

SUGGESTIONS FOR THIS WEEK

1. Write down in your journal the ways in which you don't feel good enough. Write down when that feeling first occurred. Where were you and who were you with? What decisions did you make about yourself? Write the story of that time as extensively as you can and then move into a process of forgiving yourself. If you have judged yourself as inadequate—as less than, insufficient, and lacking in some ways—remind yourself that you are as good as anyone else and you are on your way to growing, learning, and evolving.

2. Write a short letter to yourself validating all the good things about you, all the areas in your life where you are gifted and how you enrich other people's lives. Make it as extensive as possible. Acknowledge yourself for those qualities without taking them for granted.

3. How would you like your life to be a year from now? What would you like to experience differently? Pick one to three

areas where you experience a sense of lack that you would like to shift. Ask yourself what is the next action that you can take, physically, emotionally, and mentally, to start working toward this new abundant vision of self. Find someone you trust to support you in taking your next steps, and always ask for spiritual assistance; this is always available to you.

28.

LET GO OF YOUR LIMITING BELIEFS

You will become what you think about most . . . The brain simply believes what you tell it most. And what you tell it about you, it will create. It has no choice.

—Shad Helmstetter

Everything that happens in our lives is a manifestation of what we believe about ourselves and life. For example, if you think life should be hard, it will be hard. If you think that people will help you along your journey, then they will. It's very important that we examine our beliefs and challenge them in order to create beliefs that reflect what is really true for us.

I used to believe that men would disappoint me. This was rooted in how my mother felt disappointed by my father. That was the source of my belief. As an adult, I would attract men who would end up disappointing me. I call this a self-fulfilling prophecy.

One night, I was getting ready to attend a big, fancy event to which I had invited a man I was dating to accompany me, and he had happily accepted. At that time, I was living in Santa Barbara and he in Los Angeles. Thirty minutes before the event, he called to say he was stuck in traffic due to a wreck, and he wouldn't be able to make it. However unintentional it was, somehow things were set up so that this man would disappoint me. I know the reason was the traffic, but my belief that I would be disappointed was fulfilled once again.

When I told my spiritual teacher how I kept attracting men who in one way or another would let me down, he said, "When this pattern keeps recurring, you have to start asking, 'What is my belief? What am I creating and why? Where did it originate?' Who impressed this belief upon you and why did you buy into it?" Basically, he was putting the responsibility back on me. Somehow, I was creating this situation, and it was up to me to change it.

If you are one of those women who share my experience of believing that men will let us down, find out the root of your disappointment. Do you have a belief that you aren't worthy of a man who will show up for you? Or that you aren't lovable? Once you find the root, you can totally change it. I took responsibility, and I realized that I no longer wanted to be the victim and the recipient of being let down. I started to become more cognizant of who I was attracting and worked on adopting the belief that I deserved to be with good men who would show up for me. Not all men have to model my father.

Another common pattern I've observed is that people are often excluded from projects they initiated. For example, a friend of mine started a new initiative at a nonprofit and brought on a well-connected partner to support the work. They poured an extraordinary amount of thought and energy into this initiative to get it moving, but at some point, this partner began to move the project forward on her own, excluding my friend. He felt hurt, naturally, and experienced a lot of turmoil as he tried to stay involved.

He came to me for help. I asked him, "What is your belief about yourself that's creating this pattern?" He reflected and said, "I think it's egotistical if I take charge of situations, so I surrender my power. I move to the sidelines." He needed to stand his ground. Because he hadn't, he was paying the consequences. A few years later, this same friend had an idea about starting an institute, and when he caught himself ceding his leadership role, speaking as a "we" rather than an "I," he said he heard my voice say, "You are a leader. Don't surrender your power. Don't repeat the pattern. Step into the frontline; you are secondary no more. People need your wisdom and leadership."

Whatever your pattern, overcoming it requires you to feel worthy of occupying the leading role of your life. When you have the same problem over and over, you must take responsibility for having created this reality. Maybe you are running a belief that people are going to screw you over. Unearthing your limiting beliefs takes conscious awareness that somehow you are attracting these kinds of circumstances and treatments. See if you can shift that to a "lesson learned" so that you can catch yourself when you're attracting that kind of treatment again.

Let me share with you some other patterns I've observed; maybe one matches your own. My father kept entering into business relationships in which a venture—a journal, magazine, or newspaper—would almost work but, at the last minute, fall apart. In my father's world, it was always the other person's fault; his partner in the venture would do something that would totally infuriate him and break the deal. This happened over and over again. My father was a concentration camp survivor, and he saw so many of his friends killed in front of his eyes. The mark this left on him was so severe, he was never able to truly deal with it. I am certain he had a very deep sense of survivor guilt. My father had a deep belief that he didn't deserve success in the world because of everything he had witnessed, and so he would sabotage his own success.

A friend of mine used to neglect herself, helping everybody else but having no time for herself. She is a wife, mother, working woman, and a great friend. She simply didn't make time to relax or exercise, so over the years she's gained a lot of weight. One day she confessed to me, "I think I have to be all things to all people or everything will collapse. I feel a responsibility to take care of the people around me." She dug deeper. This belief was rooted in growing up the eldest of five siblings with a single working mother. She was given a lot of responsibility at a very young age, and she has carried this weight throughout her life. She was limited by the belief that she was responsible for the well-being of everyone around her, so she neglected her own. When she saw that, she started embracing the belief that she deserves to look after herself first, and she began creating healthy boundaries in how much she does for others. It took a while, but I could definitely see the difference when I saw her again. Her mental belief was being matched by the right behavior.

You might have a belief that's running your life: No one follows through; I can take care of myself and I don't need anyone else; my value is defined by my paycheck; people lie; I never get what I want; I'm not worthy, or lovable, or safe to be myself in the world. And on and on. These limiting beliefs create heaviness around your heart because they stop you from fully experiencing the abundance of your life. Each belief is, at its base, about feeling victimized and powerless. When you start to have that feeling that you're being let down by life again, remember that you are not a victim. Instead, start to heal by tracking this belief to its point of origination, and from there you can start to change it by challenging it. If you believe that men are unreliable, make a list of all the times men have been there for you. If you believe your home or workplace will fall apart without your constant attention, think about how smoothly things went that one day you were sick. Replace the lie with something more true and beneficial. As Rumi said, "Live life as if everything is rigged in your favor." This new belief will empower you, free you, and make you happier. It takes courage to look at your erroneous beliefs and claim that you are a worthy person with the ability to create your reality. Challenge the old paradigm to let in more joy, self-expansion, and well-being. Your limiting beliefs are not who you are. Life is on your side.

SUGGESTIONS FOR THIS WEEK

1. For the next week, observe how you operate in the world and how the world responds to you. Ask yourself the question "What is my belief in this situation?" What do I believe about relationships, the world, myself? Write it down with no judgments and then ask yourself, "When/where did this belief come from?" "Why did I take it on?" "What was my survival mechanism?" and "Is it really true?" Is there another belief you can adopt that is truer to who you are and can support your success, well-being, and fulfillment?

2. For twenty minutes, do free-form writing about your limiting beliefs about yourself without censoring, with the intention of releasing the source of these beliefs. Once you've finished, burn what you've written. Do this for thirty-two days, a few minutes a day. It can totally transform you as you release the unconscious, blocked energies that are restricting your self-expression and happiness. Here are some prompts to help you get started.

  ☐ Complete this sentence: In social situations, I feel _____ _____ because _____ and I would like to feel _____.

  ☐ Complete this sentence: In starting a new project/job/endeavor, I feel _____ because _____ and I would rather feel _____.

Write to your heart's content. Let go of the limiting belief and start to embrace who you are and how you would actually like to feel.

3. Do the following visualization: Imagine yourself at the age when an unhealthy belief was adopted and listen to the words people are saying around you, and to what you said to yourself. Was there a tension between your inside thought process and what the world was saying? See it, hear it with as much clarity as possible. Now, imagine yourself releasing that situation, those words, into a white light above your head, taking this thought form that has been restricting you and replacing it

with a thought you would really like to embody. Even if you don't really believe it at the moment, visualize saying it to yourself and embracing this new way of being. For example, if you have felt that the world is not a safe place, tell yourself, "I know how to be safe in the world, no matter what the world does." Visualize yourself in this new way of being, acting, and feeling. Now, take a pen and paper to jot down this vision so you can anchor a sense of worthiness and strength, and honor yourself.

29.

FIND YOUR CONFIDENCE AND BE BOLD

A ship is safe in harbor, but that's not what ships are for.

—William G. T. Shedd

I love the scene from *Chariots of Fire* in which the English runner Eric Liddell is running in an Olympic race. The runner asks himself, "Where does the power come from, to see the race to its end?" He then hears his inner voice respond, "From within."

Confidence is a by-product of that inner power that propels us to keep taking action, bypassing our fears and self-doubts. You don't have confidence when you start the race, but as you run and tap into your inner resources, it builds and takes you to the finish line. A common mistake I see is that people want to feel confident before they start anything, whether it's a job, a new relationship, living in a new place, making new friends, and so on. It doesn't happen like that. You have got to step out, risking your pride for the reward of finding your confidence.

Embarking on a new venture—starting college, a new business, a relationship, a job, or a passion project, or letting go of something that's not working for you—probably fills you with trepidation, doubts, insecurities, and fear of failure, instead of excitement. We question ourselves and fill ourselves with negative input that paralyzes us, making ourselves feel like we've failed before we've even begun. Shakespeare said it best, "Our doubts are traitors, and make us lose the good we oft might win, by fearing to attempt." When I first started working on a new project and didn't get the results I wanted, my confidence would automatically be diminished and shaken. My critical voice had to be reined in, like a wild horse that was trying to keep me from attempting anything new. The way to self-start is to cheer yourself on, conspire in your favor. That power propels you forward, undermining the doubt and the insecurities, the fears of failure and the unknown.

Look at all of these opportunities as chances to grow. Continue to learn more about your abilities, your limitations, your resilience. You don't know what you're made of until you take the plunge. Life tested me by giving me experiences that didn't match my expectations. But I also learned that I always had a choice. I could either collapse and give up on myself, or pick myself up by the bootstraps and take action, blast through my fears and find my confidence on the other side.

This hit home for me when I was cast as the housekeeper in *Surviving Picasso*, filmed in the famous Pinewood studios in London, and directed by the genius James Ivory. I'll never forget going on set, all made up and in costume, rehearsing my scene with Anthony Hopkins, who was playing Picasso. I was weak in the knees and could hardly breathe! It took a lot of guts to keep thinking, "You go, girl, you can do this." I had to support myself, 100 percent, and in that moment what happened was amazing.

Anthony Hopkins was so supportive, sensing that this was a big moment for me. He chatted with me in a lighthearted way to help me loosen up. We had such a good time doing the scene together, and at the end of shooting, he said to me, "Remember, Agapi, always be bold and mighty forces will come your way." I've never forgotten that.

Confidence is discovered beyond your comfort zones. When you break through the fear of failure and realize that it's part of the process, you'll discover that you can conquer almost anything if you keep going. Always be bold and mighty forces will come your way.

Here are the four keys to having your confidence:

1. Affirm that you are not alone. You have got to "have your back" 100 percent. Get back to connecting with your inner power. There are three ways to know you're not alone: you can reach within and grab hold of your core; you can reach outward and ask for help; and you can reach out to others and offer help.

2. Move into radical self-acceptance. Start appreciating every little thing about you, reinforcing the positive, and refrain from focusing on the negative. Write down a list of all your positive attributes. Make it as long as you can.

3. Don't wait to be perfect before you take action. You are always going to be a work in progress. Don't wait for perfect circumstances. The moment to start taking action is now. It's never too late. *The willingness to do gives you the ability to do.* Map out the next thing you would like to do and take steps

toward it, no matter how microscopic. Remember that most of the people who have been successful have had many failures along the way. Failure is a step toward success.

4. Your presence is required. Keep your heart present as you live your daily life. Make it present in your conversations, all your interactions, and everything you do.

GUIDED MEDITATION

Close your eyes. Come into a comfortable position, sitting, standing, on the floor, wherever you are comfortable and feel relaxed. Imagine being surrounded and enveloped by a golden light. This light comes from the top of your head, piercing down through your body and all the way down to your feet. It helps clears your energy, making everything clear, strong, and sharp. Start imagining yourself in all the different situations in your life: interacting with people, taking on projects that you want to complete, asking for assistance, delegating things, learning new things, being at work, at home, in relationships, going from one thing to another, attending different functions, social or professional. Visualize areas in your life where you would like to feel more comfortable with yourself, more assured, more confident. Take a look and see what might be making you feel less confident. Confidence doesn't mean that you have the answers to everything, but that you have a good sense of yourself, just the way you are. It means that you're relaxed enough to listen to your inner guidance; it means that you give yourself permission to express yourself; it means that you can be silent whenever you want to be; it means you have a sense of freedom and joy around your life, without fear of mistakes. But most important, you are at home with who you are.

Take a deep breath and imagine yourself now interacting with different people in your life. What message do you need to give yourself for you to know that you're okay just the way you are? From your higher self and intelligence, tell yourself, "I am enough in who I am. I don't have to be anything else." Start to feel a sense of gratitude about who you are, your life, all the blessings in your life, and let this gratitude fill you and lift you. Know that there is no one like you. Isn't that wonderful? There is no one like you. Make this positive statement to yourself: "I am safe, I am protected to be who I am. I love myself exactly as I am. I rejoice in the opportunity to learn new things. I give permission to myself to feel good about myself. I enjoy myself in different situations. I have a good time. I am relaxed with friends or new people—I interact with ease. I have an enjoyment of everything that's going on around my life. When I walk around in any new situation, I walk with a sense that I belong. That I am perfectly okay just the way I am." See yourself walking, grounded, expanded, not giving your power or energy away to anyone, but staying contained within yourself, giving positive statements to yourself. You tell yourself what a gift you are. You project an image of self-assurance, not overextending, not having to prove yourself but radiating from inside out. Take all of that in, and ask yourself if there is anything else that you would like to feel in the world. Give yourself that right now. You belong as much as anyone else. Visualize a lot of other people enjoying having you around, appreciating you, welcoming you because you have welcomed yourself. You are safe, you are loved, you are worthy, you are deserving. This is a new moment in your life. Take it in. Let your high self guide you every step of the way. Be you, your wonderful spirit and your wonderful self. Take a deep breath. Inhale all the way and exhale with a sound, "Ahh." Open your arms and shake your shoulders. You don't have to carry any unnecessary burdens. Isn't it wonderful to just be you? When you open your eyes, you will have a whole new sense of confidence, reassurance, and a beautifully grounded sense of you.

30.

TRUSTING YOUR CREATIVITY

Everyone is born creative; everyone is given a box of crayons in kindergarten. Then when you hit puberty they take the crayons away and replace them with dry, uninspiring books on algebra, history, etc. Being suddenly hit years later with the "creative bug" is just a wee voice telling you, "I'd like my crayons back, please."

—Hugh MacLeod

My mother used to say, "You can be creative in anything you do: washing dishes, cooking, cleaning the house, interacting with people. Creativity is an approach to life, an attitude." If I was stuck in a stupor, she'd encourage me to shift my mood and engage myself by bringing my creativity into ordinary tasks.

As grown-ups, we often relegate our creativity to our hobbies or leave it to the "masters" like Mozart, Picasso, Martha Graham, Pavarotti and Jane Austen. But you have the right to claim your own desire to sing, dance, write, build, craft, sew, organize, or decorate by simply tapping into this unknown reservoir that we have inside each of us. Suspend all judgment about who or what is supposed to be creative. When you have an idea or inspiration, always write it down. If there's still juice to move on it a few weeks later, move on it.

When I started to write my first book, *Conversations with the Goddesses*, I had an idea but wasn't clear about how to execute the vision. I started working with a mentor, a woman who had put together a lot of creative, wonderful books. She helped me structure the book and schedule the steps I had to take each week in order to complete the book. As I started to take the first steps, I felt like I was in kindergarten. I had no creative juice at that moment, but I kept performing the steps, like a procedure. Every week I would check in with my mentor and hand in my "homework." Thank God, I had a blind faith that somehow I would find my creative way.

After a few weeks of persistent work, something remarkable happened. As I dove into other books about the subject, and kept going no matter how I felt about my output, I felt a spark. I started to come up with new ideas. I saw how my take on the topic was different from Carl Jung's and the other great writers who'd written about the goddesses. I wanted to connect each goddess to a piece of literature and give each goddess a voice; because of my background in theater, I was relating the goddesses to characters in plays and giving them dramatic monologues. They started to come alive. People could actually connect with them. I felt such joy. It felt like making bread: put all the ingredients together, knead, and watch it rise.

It was one of the times I felt my creative pulse most vividly. I wrote poems for the goddesses in the middle of the night. It was like falling in love—not with a person, but with this surge of energy. I had stopped sending my mentor material for feedback. Honestly, I was so wrapped up in my own creative process that I no longer needed to ask her opinion. Weaving this material together, for me, was not a linear process, and the more I learned to go with it and trust it, the more it revealed itself to me. I started to find my voice. The more I gave myself permission to go with it, and not judge, the more creativity I found.

I've learned to have confidence that when I embark on a new project, even if I can't see the destination, I will find my way there by putting one foot in front of the other. Like an artist with a blank canvas, I don't know what's going to be there until I start to paint and it takes me somewhere I never could have dreamed.

One of the pitfalls of claiming our creativity is that we compare our work to what other people are doing. We look up to great artists, singers, painters, writers, and think "I could never match up." And why should you? Mozart did Mozart, you must do you. Your creativity is a unique divine gift, personally designed for you.

Years ago, when I was living in London, I dated an English barrister. They are stereotyped as the most intellectual, cerebral people out there. But he loved opera; we'd often go together and he would cry. He said, "I would give anything in the world to be able to sing like that." One night at dinner, I said to him, "Why don't you just take singing lessons with my teacher?" He protested, but I prevailed. Soon enough, he was taking lessons from my teacher. A year later, this wonderful man was giving a concert in a grand hall. It was a concert for his close circle of friends and colleagues. Hearing him sing, my heart began to swell from the joy I was feeling from him as he gave himself permission to express a part of himself that he had suppressed and judged as inappropriate for years.

Always give precedence to the thing that makes you feel joyful, creative, and happy. It may not be something that makes money or that other people validate. This is your gift to yourself. Do it for the love of it. This doesn't apply only to the arts, but to a new business idea, redecorating your home, a relationship that isn't predictable, traveling to an exotic land you've dreamt about, a new way to be in your marriage. All too often relationships become stagnant because we forget to renew ourselves and be creative in them. One of the happiest couples I know has been married for twenty years. The husband hides adorable little notes in unexpected places for his wife—on the wheel of her car, in her wallet, in the mail. She's a wonderful cook and surprises him with fun new dishes. These are two people who live and work together, and whenever I see them I feel that their marriage is charged with appreciation for one another.

Don't become serious about your creativity. Have you ever watched kids create? Let me share with you a story about a little four-year-old girl who was painting a picture. The teacher asked, "Who is this?" and the little girl said, "God." The teacher replied, "No one knows what God looks like," and the little girl said, "They will once I've finished." It's that kind of innocent, unabashed, bold creativity that we need to claim for ourselves.

Our very existence is creative—cells are constantly being created in our bodies, after all. Discover your particular outlet for the creativity that exists in all of us. Let it be as unique as you are, with no expectations or demands. Just return to that free and open part of you that loves to create. Go for it!

SUGGESTIONS FOR THIS WEEK

1. Look around at your life and see where your creativity needs to be rekindled. See where you've gone on automatic. Start to think of more creative ways to do things and ask yourself, "Is there another way to do this that will rekindle my creativity?"

2. Keep a pad and pen around you. Start doodling for five minutes a day; it can actually open up your creative flow and get you out of your head.

3. Go to a bookstore, a gallery, or any other place that is filled with creativity and take time to browse without an agenda, tap into the creativity of all that surrounds you, and be inspired. Join a creative class in any subject you love and let the group energy inspire you.

4. Make a list of what you used to do as a child that made you creative; whatever that was, open up your imaginary world once again. You're never too old to be creative. Dare to go there! Take back your crayons. Repeat this positive statement: I give myself permission to express the joy of my creativity.

GUIDED MEDITATION

Find a comfortable position and take a deep breath. Relax. Allow the tensions in your body to release. Come into the presence of your heart. Follow the steadiness of your breath as you inhale and exhale. Imagine a beautiful light filling you, surrounding you and protecting you.

Go back in time and remember when you were a child and you used to play freely. Maybe you dressed up in your favorite costumes or played with crayons or sculpted animals out of Play-Doh. You made mud pies outside with the mud in the garden. Remember the joy that you had as you giggled with your friends, completely unaware of what anybody thought of you. Conjure up that feeling. Make it present, right now.

Allow yourself to be filled with the joy and freedom you knew as a child. See the colors that you played with, the shapes you used to make, the abundance of being creative with abandon. Think of something you can do today that will connect you to that creative surge you had as a child. What is that for you? Is it dancing, singing, cooking, painting, writing, making crafts? Or is it gardening, arranging flowers, or acting in a play? There are hundreds of ways to be creative. What is the thing that makes your heart sing? Ask yourself what your life would be like if you gave yourself permission to connect with that original joy and freedom you had as a child, by giving yourself permission to create for the sake of creating. Bring that creative energy into your life, allowing yourself to plunge into something you want to do and infuse it with your joy.

Tell yourself, "I can totally do that. I allow myself the complete freedom to give myself my full expression and create. Being creative is my birthright."

Let go of any judgment that you may feel from yourself or others. You don't need that right now. Expressing your creativity is a gift to yourself.

Take this time to embrace your creative desire to do whatever it is that gives you joy. What is the next little thing, the next microscopic step that you need to take to start a creative project? See yourself doing it, just like that. Not a thought in your mind, just getting up and doing it. No resistance, just the flowing of your creative energy. Allow the freedom and the joy that you had as a child awaken again within you and trust the process. If you want to sing, sing.

If you want to dance, dance. Nothing has to be perfect. There are no judges and there is no competition. Freely give yourself permission to create what it is you want to create. Now see yourself having done it for a while, completing something and sustaining your creativity. See how the joy spills over to everything else you do in your life. You are a creative being. That's the truth. You don't need to be taught how to be creative because you already know how to do it.

Take a deep breath and fill yourself with the joy of your creative energy and the excitement of what you are about to start. Open your eyes, take your journal, and write down what it is you would like to do next with your creativity. Maybe even the way you write now will be more creative. Perhaps you'll use a pen you love or a colorful new journal. Or maybe as you write you will draw pictures in the margins. Just let yourself create.

Relax into your creativity and experience your joy.

31.

WHY IT'S IMPORTANT TO TELL YOUR OWN STORY

One of my favorite quotes is from Antwone Fisher, the author of *Finding Fish*, and it goes like this: "Life often has a way of making people feel small and unimportant. But if you find a way to express yourself through writing, to put your ideas and stories on paper, you'll feel more consequential. . . . Even if only one person, a family member, reads something you wrote long after you're gone, you live on. So writing gives you power. Writing gives you immortality."

You don't need to write the next *Odyssey*. Homer already did that. But it is important that you capture the moments in your life that formed you, had an emotional charge, or led you to an epiphany. Writing can take many forms: dictating to your phone and transcribing it later, posting on an online blog, writing in a notebook. Whatever supports your process, do it.

There is a thread in our lives that connects all the dots, but we can only see it when looking backwards. We all live in the unknown. But telling your stories gives you the sense that someone is watching over you. When I was writing the stories from my life in *Unbinding the Heart*, the critical part of myself would always try to censor my vulnerable stories, saying, "Don't say that. That story doesn't matter." But my heart would prompt me forward, saying, "Tell that story. Be transparent. It matters: how you found your teacher; how you let go of that relationship; how disappointments led you to redefine the meaning of success; and how closed doors led to the awareness of what you were here to do." Each story and experience became another stitch in my life's tapestry. It was awesome and tremendously healing. It was as if the curtain lifted and I was allowed to see the perfection of everything that had happened in my life: the struggles, challenges, wins, and disappointments. They were all a part of the bigger plan, leading me to find my true self. In writing your story, you will know yourself. As you share your story with others, you will become known to them.

In the process of telling my stories, I saw how the wisdom of my soul had always propelled me forward, bringing me experiences to increase my understanding and to form the perfect tapestry of my life. All the times I felt unknown, insecure, fearful, full of self-doubt were stitches in the tapestry. It takes courage to tell your story, to look at experiences that you wanted to be different. And yet, in recounting all of it, I was astounded to see that life was not against me. Life was always on my side, leading me back inside myself. The whole experience left me with greater trust, feeling more compassionate and tender toward myself, and unbound my heart.

Maybe you're thinking, "But I haven't had anything interesting happen to me." Well, how did you feel when your best friend moved away right before high school? When you broke up with your boyfriend right before your best friend's wedding? When you got your first job and realized it's not what you wanted to do? When you found out you were pregnant, or your parents separated? If something affected you, it's important. You're not writing for anyone else, so who cares what others may think? Maybe in the end you'll want to share what you wrote. It may turn out people can relate to your experience; I've been amazed by how many people have related to my journey, the story of one Greek girl's life of passions pursued and spiritual awakening. But being relatable is not what you need to focus on while writing, just focus on the joy of it!

When I finished my book, I experienced the profound feeling that my life as I had known it had ended. The story was done. It was a most liberating feeling. Also a little scary. The stories I had replayed in my head—what my parents did, what my parents didn't do, men, work, my successes and miracles—were wiped clean. I started to feel a sense of freedom, knowing that everything I had gone through had a bigger plan around it. I could see the pivotal moments when I had chosen the path back to myself. My purpose was crystallized and my trust was grounded.

If you write your story, you'll tap into the extraordinary resilience and strength that's inside of you. You will experience a catharsis. You'll have a clean slate on which to write a new narrative. You'll become the creator of your story, from that moment on.

We are all storytellers. So give yourself a chance and write your story. Just start and see where it takes you, without an agenda or goal. Don't worry about being Ernest Hemingway, Anne Lamott, or Maya Angelou. They did themselves, so you *do you*. You are worth it and your story matters. In writing your story, you bring yourself back home.

SUGGESTIONS FOR THIS WEEK

1. Over the next thirty-two days, make a commitment to start writing your story. Write in a journal, on your computer, your phone, wherever you can capture your story and whenever the mood strikes. Commit to a weekly number of entries. This practice will start the wheels churning. Write for the joy of it, not the perfection of it.

2. When you feel ready and safe, you can invite someone close to you over to share what you have written. Read it out loud to them. This will help you be known. Let yourself be seen by people who care for you.

3. If you want to capture the legacy of your life and your parents and/or grandparents are alive, you might want to videotape them and ask questions you've never asked before. This video can include interviews of siblings, teachers, and friends. It may shed light on areas in your life and bring more clarity.

32

FIND YOUR CALLING

My head is at ease knowing that what was meant for me will never miss me, and that what misses me was never meant for me.

—Imam al-Shafi'i

Michael is the son of a friend of mine—he's sixteen years old and rather evolved for his age. One day when he was visiting me, I asked him, "Michael, why do you think we are here?" and he said to me, "To wake up." When I asked him to explain a bit more, he said, "I think most people are asleep—they don't know who they are. I think we need to wake up to who we are."

He then asked me, "Agapi, why do you think we are here?" I had no hesitation: "I think we are here to evolve and transform, and I think that everything that happens in our lives, and everything that doesn't happen, is the journey to our transformation . . . I think fundamentally I agree with you, that we are here to wake up."

There is a question in all of us: What is the purpose of my life? In other words, what am I here to do? Obviously, each one of us has to find our own unique and personal answer to these questions. There is no one-size-fits-all. Finding your calling is like finding your own personal melody.

I like to think of our purpose as our individual calling. It has nothing to do with our accomplishments or our résumé; it is a deeper thing that connects us to our heart's pulse. When we find it, it adds meaning to whatever we do, and we feel purposeful and fulfilled. Not all of us are assigned to be the Dalai Lama, Mother Teresa, the Pope, or Oprah. We might delude ourselves in thinking that people who have higher visibility have a higher purpose than we do. That's not accurate at all. Your purpose doesn't have to be grandiose or world changing. We all have a purpose; connecting to it, however, is a process of discovery. And it shifts over the years. I have met thousands of people who have found purpose in some very practical, under-the-radar ways. Their job is not to be famous or be in the spotlight but to serve and better the lives of others.

When we connect to our heart's calling, everything starts to have meaning. I have come up with five questions that can bring you closer to your calling:

→ What am I here to learn?

→ What am I here to teach?

→ What am I here to overcome?

→ What am I here to complete?

→ What am I here to express?

Take a moment to answer these questions from an authentic, truthful place. Maybe write your answers in your journal. The answers may be very different from what you had expected. These questions are meant to break down self-imposed standards that bind you. Play with these questions and don't worry if your answers don't sound serious. I see these questions as a compass directing us to our center. When you are living from your center, you will enjoy your life, no matter what.

The answers to these questions are ongoing and evolving. At different stages in your life, you are here to teach and learn different things. Nothing is set in stone. As you answer these questions, you may find a blueprint emerging that can guide you to what calls you, and as you design your life according to that plan, you start to experience more of an inner fulfillment. We are all teachers and we are all students, and we all have something to contribute. That knowledge can alleviate a sense of emptiness you might feel and bring solace and comfort to you when you ask the basic question: "Why am I here?"

Being aware of your purpose will help you to expand your perspective, uncover tremendous creativity, and welcome the unknown instead of fearing it. It also puts you in the driver's seat, where we become the creator of our lives. Everything that happens in your life, the good, the bad, and the ugly, becomes part of your life's tapestry, and those experiences perform a kind of alchemy on your spirit to awaken you to who you truly are. My mother used to say, "We are all born an original, and it is a challenge to stay an original in a world that tries to mold us to fit in." Don't die a copy.

I started my life thinking that I was here to become a successful actress. I went to a prestigious drama school and was acknowledged and validated as a very talented actress. I moved to Hollywood to do a movie. When the movie did not work out, I went on a soul-searching journey only to discover, years later, that my calling was not to perform others' scripts, but to write my own life's script and create my own life. I found my calling in a New York bus performing for a stranger, realizing that I had to share my gift of expression unconditionally (see the full story in chapter 44). I had restricted myself with expectations of what life should bring me until that moment.

I waited a beat, regrouped, and dug a little deeper. I made a list of my talents and all the things I loved—I put together all the monologues from plays that inspired me and matched them to the Greek goddesses to create a one-woman show. What I realized at that moment was that I needed to be resourceful with my own talents. This means taking stock of what I'm able to do and figuring out how my abilities can create the outcome I want, let me overcome challenges, and turn struggles into opportunities.

Finding what we are meant to do with our lives, and our connection to that calling, has a lot to do with our natural abilities and gifts. Often, we don't discover these truths until we are faced with closed doors and forced to dig deeper and excavate the lost treasure of who we are and what we are truly meant to be and do. As we discover this treasure, we also discover our strength, resourcefulness, caring, tenacity, our "grit," fearlessness and our originality. This connects us with our calling. As a by-product, we find what we are here to do and how to contribute to humanity.

I often hear people say, "Breaking up with this person and going through my divorce led me to find myself and who I really was" or "Leaving the job where I was miserable led me to find out what I really wanted to do" or "Starting this new project despite my fears and doubts made me realize that I was much stronger and resilient than I thought." Know that the end of one chapter can be the beginning of you finding your calling. That has definitely been true for me throughout my life.

When I return to my home in Greece for holidays, old friends and relatives ask me if I'm enjoying my life in the States. For Greeks, joy is a big part of the meaning of life. So let me add one more fundamental question: Ask yourself, "Am I enjoying my life? And if I'm not enjoying life now, when?" It's extraordinary to think that no matter what is going on in your life, the fact that you are alive is "joy" in and of itself—because being alive means that anything is possible. This is the miracle of life.

Don't wait for anything to be different. If you are present right here and now instead of looking left and right, your calling will reveal itself. Realize that you have the ability to know your calling when you hear it. Maybe at your most difficult moment, you'll look up, exhale, and surrender, something will shift inside of you, and you'll be filled with gratitude and grace. It can happen just like THAT, if you stay open!

Think of yourself as a musical instrument that needs to be tuned daily. You are not here to just get things done, you are here to produce a beautiful sound and play your own melody. You can then do as much as you want without being spent, because you'll be riding in your own frequency and sound—your natural state of being.

What delights your heart?

SUGGESTIONS FOR THIS WEEK

1. In your journal: Make a list of all the things you love that give you joy. Make this list as expansive and thorough as you can. Not for career or accomplishment, just for joy. Look at this list often.

2. Write down an ideal scene showing what your life would look like if you were doing something that utilized all of your gifts and made a contribution to others. This can be as simple as "I'm a great listener, and I bring great comfort to people's

lives as I listen to them without judgment" or "I love helping people organize a space and bring greater clarity in their lives." Often we start to find more of our calling when we start to think about how we can contribute to the well-being of others, rather than it being all about ourselves.

3. What are some of the actions that you could take to be more proactive in doing the things you love and fully utilize your gifts?

4. What people can be a part of your support team? Share your ideal scene with these people, and ask them for help to manifest this. Be consistent about asking people for help. Look at this scene daily; rehearse it as an actual happening, not a fantasy. Make this scene as alive in your heart as possible!

33.

DEVOTED, DISCIPLINED, DISCERNING

The Magic of Triple D

There is no freedom without discipline, no vision without a form.

—David Allen

It is essential to have the qualities of discernment, discipline, and devotion in order to move forward in our lives with a sense of purpose and fulfillment.

I feel very blessed to bear witness to the way my niece, Isabella, embodies these qualities.

She's an artist, and from a young age she was very clear about what she wanted to do. She's totally devoted to her work. She spends hours and hours every day creating her art and brings the same enthusiasm to each piece. Whether she has a show or not, she doesn't stop. I watch her execute her artistry in absolute awe. There is no angst, complaints that it's hard, anxiety about becoming famous—just sheer commitment to the process. This carries her forward, day after day, piece after piece.

Discernment is the compass that shows where you want to go, discipline is the work of rowing that gets you where you want to be, and devotion is the boat that carries you forward. The three together create what I call love in action. That's the magic of 3-D.

Discernment

Discernment lets you distinguish between what is for you and what is not for you; who is for you and who is not; what to say and when to say it. Given my open and trusting nature, I have learned the wisdom of discernment through trial and error.

After recently returning to New York to live on my own and work on my book, I told a dear friend how I felt ready for someone special to come into my life. After what seemed like just a few days, this friend called and said, "There's a man I want you to meet, and I know he's the one for you. I am sure this is the man you're going to marry." No pressure! I met this man and indeed, we fell in love. I proceeded in the belief that this was the man I was going to marry. I didn't really know who he was, but wouldn't you know it, I stepped into the fantasy of what it would be like to live with him and have a life together. After six months of dating, I was already thinking about how I would redecorate his apartment and change his curtains!

A few months later, when we were coming up against challenges and the relationship was beginning to wane, I felt shattered. Wasn't this the man I was going to marry? From the get-go, I had surrendered my discernment to the fantasy. That was a really powerful lesson for me. I moved on, grieving the loss of what could have been, but accepting that it wasn't meant to be. I gained so much in knowing never to abandon my discernment due to another person's opinion of what was right for me, no matter how well intentioned.

Fundamentally, I want to like people and I want people to like me, and this used to cloud my discernment in so many ways. In business, I wouldn't do my due diligence or seek further references because I trusted that other people would take care of me. In friendships and relationships, I let people in too soon. Later, when I took off my rose-colored glasses, I didn't always like what I saw; it wasn't easy, but doing so was very empowering. I learned that some people have hidden agendas and started to trust my intuition. Over time, I asked more questions, I didn't pretend everything was fine, and I distinguished between the people I felt safe with and wanted in my inner, family-level circle and people who belonged in my friend circle. I started to listen to myself and build healthy boundaries.

Discipline

I love the word *discipline* because it comes from the word *disciple*. To be a disciple means you're in a constant state of learning, surrendering your ego and being obedient to the higher purpose.

Discernment goes hand in hand with discipline: discernment lets you partner with what is right for you, and discipline allows you to follow through; you become a disciple of what you've chosen. When I look at people I admire, I see that they share the attribute of discipline. In making anything happen in life, from taking care of your body, to having balanced emotions, to clearing your mind, to spiritual growth and personal accomplishments, you need to establish discipline. When you connect to the end result, it becomes much easier to exercise discipline every day.

I know how much it matters to me to feel healthy and vital. Exercising, eating right, and getting enough sleep come much more easily when I remind myself that the effort will let me feel the way I want. It takes discipline to give up nights out with friends and stay home to edit my new book, but knowing how pleased I'll be with the end result makes this an easier decision. Sure, there's a part of me that would rather go out and have fun than work, but this is where discernment and discipline meet.

When I was asked to write my first book about the goddesses, I embarked on an intense process of creating. It was an unfamiliar task for me. I had never written before and I didn't trust my voice, so I found a mentor who had written many books to help me structure the book. Every day I had small tasks to complete. First I had to research the seven myths and start writing about them. Then, I had to define what the archetypes meant. Day after day, I kept pouring myself into research, writing, rewriting, brainstorming. I totally immersed myself. I felt like a blind woman climbing Mount Everest in subzero conditions. But I kept going.

Six months later, when I completed my book, I felt awesome, empowered, and exhilarated. Through discipline I overcame the thought "Oh my goodness, I can never do this." I built the discipline to direct my mind toward a positive future outcome and keep thinking, "Yes, I can do this." What really activated my discipline was my devotion to expressing the wisdom that I felt in my heart about these archetypes. I knew that with this book, I was going to have a bigger vehicle to express my creativity, something I so longed for.

Devotion

A lot of people *start* to meditate: they do it a few times, it doesn't click right away, and they let their practice dwindle. You don't connect with the divine on day one, after all. They lose the devotion—they don't feel that spark—and therefore lose the discipline.

Devotion gives you enthusiasm. It's that deeper thing in you. There is so much you can overcome when you have connected with your devotion, and you find ways to reach your goals. Often we are not prepared to put in the hours it takes to get the results we want. Underneath it all, we haven't felt the value of what we'll gain by maintaining our discipline. That's a kink in the chain. Sometimes the kink is that we're spoiled; we want it now and on our terms. Instant gratification. The hard truth is there are no shortcuts to achieving anything meaningful. Devotion is the love of something that will give you the discipline to achieve it. I see a lot of people who lose discipline because they have not anchored their devotion.

Later in my life, after I had completed my work on the goddess archetypes, I had a deep desire to help people and tell them how I had found my path, my connection to myself—how I overcame challenges and learned the value of keeping my heart open. In order to reach many people, I needed to first write my story, in detail, and share with people how I found my life's calling. The devotion I felt to helping others unbind their hearts and find their calling gave me the discipline I needed to complete my book.

Once my book was published, and I had authentically told my story, I was able to speak to others in a very connected way, and they were able to unlock spaces in their hearts that were closed. The exchange of heartfelt connections and life stories that I have encountered in my work is priceless.

SUGGESTIONS FOR THIS WEEK

1. Take an inventory of your life and look at the areas where you did not listen to your discernment. Write them down. Where did you ignore the red flags? Was there something that you

knew better, but you bypassed your higher wisdom? What was the price you paid? What was the lesson you learned?

2. Is there an area in your life where you could apply more discipline? Is it your body, your work, your food, your sleep, your devices, your tidiness, your spending, your time management? Pick an area where you could be more disciplined. Lovingly support yourself in implementing microsteps to get where you want to be. No judgments, just daily action.

3. Awaken your devotion. Ask yourself, "What really matters to me?" Take a moment and come into your heart, and be honest: Why does this particular area matter to me? What is the benefit I will gain as I accomplish this particular endeavor? How much do I value myself to know that being devoted to what I love to do is paramount to my fulfillment? Breathe it in, all the way to your heart, and know that your devotion is connected to the deeper root of your spirit. When all of you is 100 percent fully engaged in your life, you feel awake, present, connected, and capable of anything.

34.

IT'S NOT A TRADE, IT'S AN OFFERING

Giving is a shortcut to happiness.

—Arianna Huffington

Have you ever heard of "Greek hospitality"? Or better yet, experienced it? In our culture, we are notorious for offering our hospitality to strangers. I have heard so many stories from friends who visit the Greek isles about being invited into a local's home for dinner. If you find yourself joining a Greek family for dinner and, perhaps, admire a pretty cup, the hostess will probably say, "Take it with you." That generosity can fill you with the warmth of life and a feeling of home, no matter where you are.

Whenever someone visited my family's home when I was young, whether it was a dear friend or a new neighbor, my mother would always say, "What can I offer you?" I remember one night my mother wore a beautiful pearl necklace to dinner with some friends. During the meal, a woman my mother had just met admired her necklace. Instantly, without a second thought, my mother unhooked the necklace and placed it in the woman's hands, saying, "Here, take it, now it is yours." The woman was amazed and reluctant to take the necklace. She said, "I wish I had something to give you in return." My mother said, "But, my dear, it's not a trade, it's an offering!"

Classic Mom! When we got back home, my sister and I asked her why she did that. "My darlings," she said, "there is no explanation for such a thing. It is given in the moment, in the spirit of offering." This virtue of "radical generosity" has stayed with me ever since I was a little girl. Following my mother's example, I, too, have done things for others in a spontaneous, joyful, and somewhat random way. The reward is priceless. I have also been a recipient of other people's unconditional offerings, and it has had a profound effect on my life.

Just the other day, I received a selfless offering. It was raining heavily as I was coming out of a meeting in New York City, looking for a taxi, and I noticed there was a lady already waiting for one. After a little while, with no taxi in view, she turned to me and said, "Would you like to share the next taxi that comes?" "I'd be delighted," I replied, and within seconds, a taxi appeared and we both got in. We ended up having the most wonderful conversation. Mine was the first stop, and when I grabbed my purse to pay my share, she refused to take any money and said, "This is on me. You can get the next one for someone else." I felt like I was in the cab with my mom. What a stunning moment of offering! It changed my day.

I'm always hearing about "empowerment," people looking to connect with their own power, uncover their hidden potential. I believe there's a simple and immediate way to empowerment: look inside yourself and tap into your place of "radical generosity"— make an offering! It's profound how life thanks you for your offering. If you want to be lifted, lift someone else. It's the quickest way to know your best self and, ultimately, your power.

Remember that these offerings don't need to be material:

offer your goodness, offer your knowledge, offer your humor—
and, above all, offer with your heart. When we genuinely offer
with our hearts, our hearts experience oneness and connection
with others. This kind of spontaneous offering is not something
you schedule or plan—it's a response. You see someone with a
need and you help to fill it. That intention behind the action is
what makes it an offering.

When and where can you make such offerings, you might ask?
Anywhere. Anytime. Offer a smile or a kind word to someone
who seems upset or down. Offer your empathy and wisdom to
friends and coworkers who are experiencing difficulties. Offer a
compliment to the person next to you on the subway. Talk to
someone at a party who doesn't know anybody. Help someone
on a plane struggling to fit bags in the overhead compartment.
Connect a young student to career opportunities. Cook a meal
for the family of someone who is recovering from surgery. Offer
your time with no expectation of repayment. There are endless
opportunities to be of service! This will fill your heart with joy and
delight you.

A friend of mine shared a wonderful story of how a well-timed,
generous offering deeply affected her. After a sudden breakup
and weeks of stressful apartment hunting, my friend finally found
a place and quickly moved in—only to discover that the new bed
she had bought was badly damaged. Frustrated and overwhelmed,
she mentioned this to her new landlord. To her great surprise, her
landlord offered to drive her to the store to exchange the broken
furniture, and even offered to take her grocery shopping. She
asked her landlord how she could make it up to her, and the landlord replied, "Don't even think of it. I was happy to help—this is
just how I like to do things."

Find a way to be generous today. Surprise someone! Be generous with your heart! You will feel more connected and enriched. I truly believe that if you live in a state of offering—even if you think you have nothing to give—life blesses you and you feel abundant, more at peace with who you are and what you have. You'll realize how much you already have. Your cup will overflow.

SUGGESTIONS FOR THIS WEEK

1. Every day this week, find situations and moments where you are in a state of offering. Have a clear intention in the morning that today will be a day of offering. Surprise and delight yourself with what opportunities come your way. Replace the thought "What can I get?" with "What can I give?" Write down in your journal what happens and how you feel after these interactions.

2. Open yourself to receiving offerings. Notice how wonderful spontaneous moments of offering by others are too. Allow others to give to you. Don't block it—even if it is just a nice compliment. Don't ever discount the positive words and good things that others extend to you. Receive them.

3. Take a day when you realize how much life is freely offering to you: your breath, your ability to move, to see, everything around you functioning and working without you having to do anything. You turn on the faucet and water comes out; the bus gets you safely to work; you go to the supermarket and there are fresh fruits and vegetables of every kind, you flip a switch and the room lights up. There is SO much in your life, so be in awe of how much is offered to you daily. Don't ever take it for granted.

35.

TAKE A SABBATICAL FROM HAPPINESS

Be happy, not because everything is good,
but because you see the good in everything.

—Dale Partridge

If you Google the word *happiness*, hundreds of millions of links pop up, offering different tips, behaviors, and practices to help you become happier. Oddly, the longing for happiness seems to increase the more we search for it.

I want to shed some light on a different way to look at the subject of happiness that might free us from the pressure to find it. For most people, happiness is a feeling that floods us when something positive happens in our lives. But with this definition, we become dependent on circumstances outside of ourselves and out of our control to make us feel good.

The Greeks have a word for the state of happiness called "euphoria." The noun form is *euphoros*, which literally means "the bearer of goodness." One of the essential elements in finding euphoria is to be the *euphoros*—the bearer of goodness—for yourself and for others. So instead of endlessly searching for happiness externally, what if we were to start seeing ourselves as a bearer of goodness? This means radical generosity, starting with yourself. Unlocking euphoria begins with thinking good thoughts, express- ing good feelings, and bringing goodness into your life and the lives of others with good actions. An amazing thing happens when you decide to be the bearer of your own goodness. You become a magnet that attracts good things and good people to your life. You will start to realize that life is actually "rigged in your favor," and you will naturally experience happiness without having to seek it.

I believe we are all born with innate goodness. Think back to your childhood—you probably had that effervescent exuberance and joy, not at all questioning who you were, but spontaneously living in the authenticity of you. Over the years, though, you started to restrict this unabashed way of expressing yourself. Maybe your parents censored you; your teachers reprimanded and criticized; young love went awry; your classmates might have bullied you. When this happens, you start to lose the connection to your inherent goodness. You lose your sense of safety in the world, and you judge your value as a human being. You think to yourself, "If these things are happening to me, then I must be bad and not deserving of good things." So you form a crust around your goodness and the world becomes harsh.

You start to chase happiness in accomplishments, in looking for love, possessions, and material success, but happiness can still elude you because you might be missing the golden thread that weaves together the goodness in your life. When we lose our sense of goodness, we lose our sense of self-worth, and life feels futile. But when we know our goodness, every little thing in life has meaning and we are filled with happiness.

For me, a lot of my self-doubts came from my parents'

separation. I was suffering watching my parents suffer, and that caused me a lot of unhappiness. Because things looked bad, life was lacking goodness and this made me question my own goodness. My joy was dimmed, my unhappiness escalated, and this impacted my life.

So I looked for happiness elsewhere since I couldn't find it in myself: my acting career, men, recognition for my work. When these things didn't bring me happiness, I had to return to myself. What helped me to rediscover my goodness was doing the inner work and letting go of the unhappy imprints of my story. There were a lot of layers to get past, many of which I worked through in writing my memoir *Unbinding the Heart*. I rediscovered deeper parts of my goodness, joy, and forgiveness, and that allowed me to assist others along their journey of self-discovery. That brought me a lot of happiness. When you rediscover your goodness, it flows out and spills over to every aspect of your life, enriching other people's lives.

So my advice to you is to take a sabbatical from being happy or unhappy. It's too much pressure, and it's making us narcissistic and self-absorbed, cutting off the circulation to our happiness. As Socrates said, "The unexamined life is not worth living." So get off the happiness treadmill and dig a little deeper. Happiness is an inside job. Don't pursue happiness; just let go of beliefs that have constricted your true nature as a bearer of goodness, and happiness will come. No matter what happened to you in the past or is happening to you now, you are good. Good people do good things, create good, and bring good. Imagine if you woke up one day and said to yourself, "I am a bearer of goodness, and I see the good in everything and everyone, including myself." You are bound to get very happy very fast!

So practice this mantra: "I am good, therefore I am happy."

You will infuse the environment around you with your goodness, and you will experience how the world around you starts to favorably respond. You will attract good things into your life, and you will land in happiness without even thinking about it. This, my dear friends, is the secret to your happiness.

GUIDED MEDITATION

Wherever you are, at the office, at home, in the parking lot, just take a few moments to attune to your own breath, the inhalation and exhalation. Relax your shoulders, your neck, and take a few moments to imagine that your breath is like a wave that comes in and goes out. Its cyclical movement embraces your whole body, from your toes to the top of your head, up and down, in and out. Imagine that this cyclical wave of your breath that's harmonious and balanced and euphoric has no sense at all of constriction, of restriction, but beautifully flows around you. Place a wave of calmness in your breath so that every time you're breathing in, you're breathing a deeper calmness. Every time you're breathing out, you go deeper into the calmness. You're riding this wave of calmness that's bringing you great happiness and euphoria. Send this wave of calmness to the day ahead of you, whatever is going on, project it into your day, project it into your world, project it into your thoughts, into your future. Seeing everything around you being filled with this wave of calmness, grounded in your goodness. See yourself calm and centered, and affirm, "I am a bearer of goodness. Goodness inside and out. Wherever I go, my good meets me as I return to the goodness of myself." Let this now radiate out of you like a magnetic field starting to attract goodness. Anchor this in your heart and belly, and with this beautiful field of energy around you, with a smile on the inside and out, open your eyes. Wriggle your toes and fingers, shake your shoulders, and come back to the present. Take one more deep breath, and as you exhale, extend your arms and open yourself up to all of this goodness that awaits you.

36.

DON'T SIDESTEP YOUR EMOTIONS

Our wisdom is all mixed up with what we call our neurosis. Our brilliance, our juiciness, our spiciness, is all mixed up with our craziness and our confusion, and therefore it doesn't do any good to try to get rid of our so-called negative aspects, because in that process we also get rid of our basic wonderfulness.

—Pema Chodron

What do you do when your colleague gets the promotion you wanted and feelings of jealousy and hurt surface? When you're waiting to hear from a company where you interviewed? How about when your significant other forgets to acknowledge your birthday? How do you feel when your friend lies to you? How do you cope with an elderly parent? How do you deal with the emotions that surface in these difficult moments? I've discovered that the challenge isn't actually the feelings on their own, but how we judge them. We get upset that we are upset, and that makes things so much harder. The quickest way to support yourself is to immediately own these feelings, accept them, and say to yourself, "I will not bypass this journey."

I was very fortunate to be born in a culture that encourages the freedom to express your feelings. If you ask a Greek how he is doing, he'll never say, "Fine." I actually don't think this word exists in the Greek vocabulary. Instead, he'll tell you exactly how he feels, whether he's excited, happy, sad, grateful, depressed, worried, overwhelmed, or furious. Why say you're fine when you know you aren't? It's so much more powerful to stay connected to your feelings and express them as they surface.

I have witnessed many people on their spiritual path, myself included, who judge their negative feelings as unspiritual. A spiritual person *can't* feel jealous, hurt, or angry, they tell themselves. So they pretend they are okay, great even, and attempt to bypass negative feelings. This denial can cost you your authenticity and leave you disconnected from yourself.

Remember how you'd just cry your eyes out when you were little? If Mom or Dad would immediately try to shut you up, even spanking you sometimes, saying, "Stop crying," you grew up censoring your emotions. I lived for many years pretending my feelings didn't exist. I felt too vulnerable to express them, and I didn't feel I had a safe place to emote. So, what did I do? I tried to eat them away. I discovered that rum raisin ice cream could be a great pacifier. Unfortunately, ice cream is not a long-term solution. I might have been soothed for a minute, but over time my energy would sink and I would find it difficult to be productive. My energy was pulled toward that locked emotion. I remember walking around feeling like I had a beehive in my stomach. It became so debilitating that I decided to use these emotions, however uncomfortable, for my growth.

Even a minor incident can lead to an epiphany if you let your emotions be your teacher. I introduced two friends who were both in the art world, thinking that knowing each other would enhance their work. Weeks later, one of those friends asked me if I was going to the other's dinner. I felt my stomach drop because

I hadn't been invited. I was the one who introduced them! On the outside, I pretended it didn't matter because I was too proud. Inside, I was hurt.

This feeling of exclusion had surfaced before. Not just socially, but professionally and romantically. I wanted to find the root of this pattern: Where did it come from? How was I allowing this feeling to reoccur? I think we set ourselves up to experience specific pains as many times as necessary to show us something that needs to be healed inside. When I looked honestly into this feeling of exclusion, I found an adolescent emotion dating back to my parents' separation, when I was unable to express my pain, and the excruciating loneliness translated into a sense of exclusion. I yearned to feel included and connected, and started to become dependent on others accepting me, including me, and validating me. This need continued for years.

I gave myself a lot of permission to explore the roots of my negative feelings: hurts unaddressed, powerlessness, jealousy, loneliness. I started to experience and feel them, and release the judgment. As I gave myself permission to feel vulnerable, experience my own loving, and embrace that part of myself, I started to heal. I felt a tremendous sense of freedom and happiness.

It's easy to blame other people for our hurt feelings. But you're not a victim. When you take responsibility and ownership for how you feel, it's easier to let go. Examine where, how, and when you allowed your feelings to get hurt. Negative feelings are a golden opportunity to heal what's been locked inside of you. Cry if you need to, yell, stomp your feet, just express them any way you want. Researchers have found that when we cry, our tears actually contain cortisol, the stress hormone. Crying actually diminishes stress. I highly recommend taking acting classes; there are so many characters that can help you express what you're going through when words just don't cut it. Friends are also a great comfort. Those friends who make you feel safe to admit how you are feeling. When my friends shared their own feelings of sadness, anxiety, or hurt with me, I used to want to make things better for them, but now I allow them the space to express themselves. I don't try to "fix" their experience. It's a great gift to allow your friends their process.

As uncomfortable as our negative feelings can be, they deserve our attention and compassion because they hold keys to our spiritual transformation. Don't bypass them, but also don't put them in the driver's seat. They belong in the passenger seat, where you can see and talk to them as you go through the tunnel. Remaining in the driver's seat yourself will help you emerge on the other side calm, steady, and clear.

So, here are some of the ground rules to help you handle your feelings:

1. There is nothing wrong with you for having these feelings. Do not judge yourself for feeling the way you feel. Accept them.

2. Learn to express your feelings as soon as they come up. Affirm them: "I give myself permission to feel this way." Do not manipulate yourself to feel differently.

3. Forgive any judgment of your current emotional state. For example, "I forgive myself for judging myself for feeling sad" (or left out, hurt, disappointed, depressed, etc.).

4. Ask yourself, "Can I trace this feeling to its root?" See if any images or memories come to mind. If you discover the root, make sacred time to go through what you need.

5. Ask yourself, "What do I need to do to help myself let go of these feelings?"

GUIDED MEDITATION

Find a comfortable place to sit for a few minutes where you won't be distracted. Take a slow, deep breath and exhale. As you breathe in, come into a centered place inside yourself, observing the rising and falling of your breath. Bring into your awareness a time when you experienced uncomfortable feelings. Maybe you felt hurt, discounted, ignored, or rejected. Maybe something happened where you didn't feel important, heard, or simply loved. Is there something you keep feeling over and over again that has your attention, but you haven't been able to address it? Is there some emotion you keep feeling over and over again that has your attention but you haven't been able to address it? What would you like to feel instead and how can you release and forgive the emotion that is depleting you?

Bring your awareness now to that unhappy emotion and start to deeply breathe into that tight place, that place that has closed down and perhaps created a knot in your belly or heart. Give yourself permission to absolutely experience what you are feeling. Tell yourself, "I give myself full permission to feel the way I feel." What words come up? Complete these sentences: I feel like . . . I am upset because . . . I am unhappy because . . . I am worried that . . . I am afraid that . . . I feel angry because . . . I don't feel loved and appreciated because. . . .

Take your right hand and place it on your belly, and

place your left hand on your heart, and say, "[Your name], I am here for you. I hear you. I understand how you feel. It must be difficult to experience these emotions. But it's all okay." Recall a time when you felt this way at an earlier stage in life, maybe during childhood or early adulthood. Bring that memory into your consciousness. How you feel now trumps these previous feelings. This is the time to own it, experience it, and start to forgive yourself for feeling it.

Complete these sentences: I forgive myself for judging myself for feeling upset about . . . I forgive myself for judging myself for having these feelings of . . . I forgive myself for judging the person who has caused this disturbance. Forgive the judgments and let it go. Do this as many times as you need. Observe the pain of your feelings from the first time you felt this way until now. Bring up as many memories as you can. As they come up, keep the stream of consciousness on forgiveness. If you find that you're holding on too tight, or being righteous or vindictive, keep forgiving.

Take your time, and start to experience a beautiful, calm wave of light entering your belly. Fill your heart with a loving energy that is compassionate, understanding, and absolutely loves you, like a mother loves her child. Ask yourself, "What can I do for you to help you move forward and let go of these feelings? What would you like from me? Is there something you want to express to someone? Are there any tears that need to be shed?" It's all okay. Fill yourself with a sense of openness and let your heart soften, and know that sometimes things happen in our lives that can be disturbing. But now you have a tool, assistance, and support. Let your breath widen, slow down, and bring in an image of wholeness: the sun beaming in your heart; a beautiful, abundant garden; a waterfall; birds flying in the sky; happy butterflies in your stomach, freeing up all energies. Know that you are loved no matter what. Make this process totally okay. Be calm. Be centered. Be grounded. Be forgiving of yourself and others. Open your arms and give yourself a big hug. Take yourself in, all the way, and say, "I love you, no matter what." Take a deep breath now and gently open your eyes and return to this physical reality; wriggle your fingers and toes; stretch your neck left and right; shake your shoulders; take a deep breath and exhale with a sound, "Ahh!"

Send a wave of light into your day, asking that only good meets you. Remember that things might come up, but that's okay because you now have the golden key to forgiveness and to loving yourself. Gradually become present in the room. Wriggle your hands and feet, stretch your neck, take a deep breath and open up your arms to embrace this new feeling of balance. When you are ready, stand, and make sure you drink some water before you move to ground yourself. Smile, inside and out. Why not?! You are alive, you are well, and you are on your way to knowing how wonderful you are.

37.

WHICH WOLF WILL YOU FEED?

The greatest weapon against stress is our ability to choose one thought over another.

—William James

An old Cherokee was teaching his grandson about life. "A fight is going on inside me," he said to the boy. "It is a terrible fight, and it is between two wolves. One is evil—he is anger, envy, sorrow, regret, greed, arrogance, self-pity, guilt, resentment, lies, false pride, ego, and feelings of inferiority or superiority." He continued, "The other is good—he is joy, peace, love, hope, serenity, humility, kindness, benevolence, empathy, generosity, truth, compassion, and faith. The same fight is going on inside you—and inside every other person, too."

The grandson thought about it for a minute and then asked his grandfather, "Which wolf will win?" The old Cherokee simply replied, "The one you feed."

It's quite empowering to know that we are the ones who feed the wolves and choose which wolf thrives. What do these two wolves represent? It's none other than our positive or negative self-talk. One is the part that undermines us by telling us that other people are better, smarter, or luckier, the part that gets jealous or feels angry when we don't get our way. Those negative thoughts will drain the energy from your mind and body. The other voice is self-supportive, loving, forgiving, kind, compassionate, and stands by us no matter what.

Let's take envy, for example. Maybe it comes up when you see someone else succeed, enjoy fulfilling relationships, earn recognition. As an actress, I wasn't getting the parts I wanted in Hollywood, and I constantly compared myself to others. One of my turning points came when I was writing my first book, about the goddesses. It was Oscar season and I was watching the show with a few of my friends. That year, Gwyneth Paltrow won the Oscar for *Shakespeare in Love*. Now remember, I was trained as a classical Shakespearean actress and had played the part of Viola in Shakespeare's *Twelfth Night* in England. So there she was in her stunning pink dress, looking pure and young, at the prime of her success, holding her Oscar, and I got a knot in my stomach and thought, "Why not me?" There I was, writing my first book, being given a tremendous opportunity, but I wanted the kind of recognition she was getting. I was happy for Gwyneth, and I didn't want to be Gwyneth; I just wanted to be Agapi and have my own opportunities to express myself.

I woke up the next morning with a sense that my bad wolf was really winning. I was feeding him. The more I thought about it, the worse I felt. The irony is that I was writing a book about goddesses who were mighty and powerful and never compared themselves to one another. Aphrodite never wanted to be Athena, and Athena never wanted to be Aphrodite. Each one was the best for the role she was playing.

Something happened in me that night. I picked myself up and

told myself, "Why are you doing this to yourself? You know better. You don't want to be Gwyneth Paltrow, and you don't want her path. You have your own. You are following your path, which is beautifully marked and divinely directed." I had to exorcise that part of myself, which was hurting me and snuffing out my light. From then on, I started to feed my good wolf: my talents, courage, creativity, uniqueness, Greekness. I looked in the mirror and said, "Listen to me, there is one Agapi in this world, and this role has been assigned to me. God bless Gwyneth Paltrow and her roles and awards. She got that part. But I have to live in my own skin and let my energy shine. And that's that." I think my bad wolf got really scared and started to back away. My starving good wolf started to grow stronger, more vibrant, and energized.

However, I always have to watch because the bad wolf tries to sneak in. The game is won with vigilance. For a while I stopped reading magazines because the images of fame and glamour were triggering negative self-talk. I replaced them with the self-supportive habit of reading uplifting and nurturing books.

When it comes down to it, you have a finite amount of energy and you shouldn't waste it. Stay purposeful about your thoughts. There is a cliché phrase: Be your own best friend. That's good, but I think you also need to be your best cheerleader. Whatever we say to ourselves, our body and mind hear it. So we need to be conscious of what we are saying and how we shut down our heart when we compare ourselves to others. This comparison makes us very sad.

Keep feeding the good wolf. He will be ever loyal, protect you, warm you, and be your guardian. With him, you will feel supported, strong, and feisty.

GUIDED MEDITATION

Sit in a comfortable position. Take a deep breath. Exhale with a sigh, "Ahh." Take another deep breath and become present in your heart. Start to scan your field of energy. How are you feeling inside? How's your head? How's your heart? How's your belly? How do you feel in your energy? Do you feel strong, alive, directed, and purposeful?

If not, can you follow the thoughts you are feeling that don't allow you to feel this way? Are they your thoughts, other people's thoughts? Energies from others can start to affect the way you feel about yourself. Start to track those energies. Make a note of them. Start to really identify what you tell yourself about your life that's not necessarily true.

Imagine at the top of your head a bright light that's filling you up from head to toe, like a warm light shower. Imagine that those thoughts are being transmuted by light. Little by little, start to push away from the top of your head any thoughts or energies that don't support you, any critical self-talk, any part of you that feels disconnected. As you push it away, start to replace it with thoughts of joy, hope, possibilities. Now start to scan your energy field again and experience the shift. Is your heart feeling more open and relaxed? Do you feel more connected to yourself? Distance yourself from the thoughts of other people who you compare yourself to and watch them pass by as if you're watching a film. Those thoughts have no power over you anymore. Know that you are whole and complete. When you think of the future, project all the things you do and all the things you want to do, project thoughts of lightness, openness, and of new things.

Send a big message to yourself: "Good things are meant to come my way and I allow them and receive them." In this moment of receptivity, take a moment to fill yourself with newness, knowing that the old is gone. You're giving yourself a new internal dialogue: a kinder, softer, more compassionate way of being. Take a deep breath and bring this newness into your belly, into your heart, into your whole body, all the way down to your feet, circling back to your head until you are enveloped by this positive field of energy. Very gently open your eyes and stay in this frame of mind. Move your neck, left and right. Wriggle your fingers and toes. Roll your ankles. Shake your shoulders. Take a deep breath, open your arms and exhale, and wrap your arms around, giving yourself a big hug. And smile inside and out.

38

FOUR MAGIC WORDS: CAN YOU HELP ME?

Life doesn't make any sense without interdependence. We need each other and the sooner we learn that the better for us all.

—Joan Erikson

Have you ever felt stuck? I have. I've been stuck many times, not knowing what to do next because things didn't work out. Stuck in relationships I didn't know how to end. Stuck emotionally or wanting to make something happen and not knowing where to begin.

We all need help in different areas of our lives. From health to finances, careers, relationships, parenting, and social life, or practical things like getting the best deal in a new car or finding a good plumber, we all need help. There are four magic words that have almost always opened the door to the solution I'm looking for: "*Can you help me?*" It's profound what happens when we open up and ask for assistance, allowing solutions and grace to be available to us. To quote a favorite Bible passage, "Ask and you shall receive."

As a young girl I watched my mother ask for help in so many areas of her life. She had left my father and pretty much raised me and my sister on her own. Her love and passion for us made her bold about asking for help whenever she needed it. I think she was so confident about asking for help because fundamentally she was a giver. She helped so many people. Asking and receiving, giving and helping were part of her circle of life. She was extremely gracious about the way she asked and had no shame about it.

When I was fifteen, I wanted to go to the Royal Academy of Dramatic Art in England, and she proceeded to ask everybody she knew if they knew somebody who had gone to that drama school until she found the right person. She then tracked that person down, got the contact information she needed, and found me the best teacher in London, who I then studied with and who helped me audition for the Academy. From my mother, I learned who to ask, how, and when, without being pushy or inappropriate.

But I was always more comfortable giving and helping others than asking for and receiving help. I had to teach myself the good habit of asking for help. When I was producing my first PBS special on the goddesses and had no idea how to make it happen, I started to ask people who had produced before for PBS to guide and show me, and to introduce me to people at the broadcasting company. I used to put a lot of pressure on myself to do things alone, but when I gave myself permission to admit that I needed help and asked for it, I found that other people—and the entire world—became my allies. By practicing and trying, I learned who to ask, how to time it, and how to not take it personally when I got a no. I also learned to give other people permission to decline. Let go of the idea that you know it all and can do it all on your own. Living this way is a very constricting and egocentric position that blocks you from receiving grace. So why not open up to the power of connected living? Once you live that way, asking for help will become much easier.

Asking is the gateway to receiving. I often ask people what it is that blocks them from asking for assistance, and the answers vary. Some people say that they are afraid they will be rejected and they reject themselves before they even ask for help, assuming the answer will be no. Some people say they're too proud and don't want to appear vulnerable. Some people simply don't feel worthy of being helped. Others don't want to appear needy or don't want to impose on others. There are others who feel they would give up their independence if they asked for help. If you can believe it, some have said to me they don't feel they need any help!

Have you ever noticed how much easier it is to ask on behalf of other people? We have no problem asking for a friend who is in need. Think about why you'd rather ask for a friend than for yourself. Next time you're about to ask for help, think of yourself as someone you hold dear, and see if the asking becomes easier.

Think of it this way. When we receive help, we free up our energy to make us more available to give of ourselves and to make a contribution to the world. Part of the reason I think my mother was so free in asking was because the undercurrent of her life was service. In her own way, she was always serving others. To her, it was almost second nature to help herself in order to help others, and she felt that's what life was about, the circle of love.

The truth is we're all interconnected. As William James said, "We are like islands in the sea, separate on the surface but connected in the deep." No matter who we are, we rely on the help of others. It's a myth to think that we can do it all alone. If you are one of those people who believe you don't need any help, counsel your ego not to be so threatened when asking for help and help it mature by discovering the joy of asking.

When you want help with something look at it as an adventure in finding the people who can help you get what you want. Your ego always wants to feel in charge, it wants to protect itself and not expose the fact that you don't have all the answers. It's hard, but you need to surrender your ego so your pride doesn't isolate you from others, making you feel alone. There's no sense in feeling this way when help is just a question away: "Can you help me?"

Here's what you do. First, turn inward and say, "Please help me" to that part of you that is divine, that is your spirit. Ask, "Who do you suggest I ask for help in this matter? Who shall I reach out to? Who can shed some light for me?" You will hear an answer from the wise part of yourself. Give yourself this gift. It might feel awkward, but how wonderful it is when you start to free yourself up and train yourself not to collapse in discouragement and instead keep going. How splendid it is when miracles start to happen and your universe starts giving you ample assistance in every area.

Start to anticipate the joy that comes with asking. Move out of your comfort zone and stand up for yourself, dare to ask, and know that the freedom of asking will give you a sense of your larger self.

SUGGESTIONS FOR THIS WEEK

➻ Ask for help in any area in your life where you could use it. Notice how comfortable or uncomfortable you feel. Notice any nervousness you might feel in asking and observe it. Write down in your journal your experiences, your feelings, and your thoughts.

- Practice asking from your heart, and put your love into asking with gratitude and appreciation for the other person who might be able to assist you. Give that person the opportunity to serve you in this particular area. Heartfelt gratitude is the key to asking and receiving.

- Notice where you're coming from when you're asking. Are there any judgments for feeling needy, in lack, selfish, or like you're not worthy of being helped? Reframe these beliefs and celebrate the joy of asking and the sense of openness and freedom it can bring you. Record your experience in your journal as you shift from the fear of asking to the liberation of receiving.

39.

FINDING GRACE IN DISAPPOINTMENT

Whenever I'm speaking in front of people I ask, "How many of you have experienced disappointment in your life?" Every hand is raised—if not, it's because the person didn't hear me. I've never met anyone who has not had the experience of disappointment. Disappointment comes in many shapes and colors. But the theme is always the same: expectations not being met.

One of the bigger disappointments I've experienced occurred when I was preparing a production for a movie on Maria Callas based on my sister's biography of her. It was a project that was very dear to my heart, and I had a great partner who had put a lot of money into it. We had hired a famous Italian director, a wonderful actress, and a tremendous crew. After endless meetings with the writers and producers, the director abruptly left the project and took on another film. Later he decided that he wanted to do the Maria Callas movie on his own—write it, produce it, and direct it himself.

The day I received this news, I felt my whole world had crumbled. I had invested so much in this movie. It had been such a huge part of my life; I thought it would launch my career as a producer. But there was nothing I could do. Because the director lived abroad, it wasn't practical to sue, dispute, or combat what he'd done, so I was left with tremendous feelings of betrayal. I experienced the full gamut of emotions expressed in the Greek tragedies.

Everything shifted when, one day, my mother said to me, "Darling, you have been playing the disappointment channel for too long. It's time to change the channel." I did. I let it go and moved on. *I changed the channel.* When I finally let it go, I felt amazing. The experience taught me so much about how I set myself up for disappointment. There were many signs and red flags about this director that I had ignored. I was so seduced by his talent and fame and my wishful thinking that my dream was coming true. But the lesson I learned was priceless.

Fundamentally, we are wired by human nature to have expectations. You want things to work out a certain a way, *your way.* You plan and imagine the desired outcome and attach your own fantasies to the experience. You tell yourself stories about how things should happen, and when the reality does not match, you feel let down and experience a loss of energy.

Disappointment can show up in every area of life. For example, often we project what we think a relationship should be like, how we should be treated and loved. When your partner does not meet your expectations, you are disappointed. It can be as simple as going to a movie that everyone says is wonderful—and then it's not. Or you go out for an evening with friends thinking you're going to have a good time, but you end up hurt by a thoughtless comment or feeling left out. Dating is one of the ultimate occasions for disappointment. It seems like nine times out of ten our dates do not match our expectations. What about work? Raising money for projects, looking for new clients, taking endless meetings, and thinking things will materialize, but they don't. Or a job interview. When I was auditioning as an actress, I'd go after roles that I thought were right for me, but I still wouldn't get the parts. My vision and the casting director's did not match. I didn't understand that at the time and felt rejected. I was filled with discouragement and disappointment.

When going for a job interview, you tell yourself, "I know this is the job for me, I'm perfect for it." You visualize getting the job, which builds your excitement. You listen to what you tell yourself and start to believe it. Then, the person interviewing you just doesn't get you. She is cold and aloof, maybe she takes calls in the middle of the meeting. She looks down at your résumé, she looks up at you and, in a monotone voice, says, "Thank you so much, we'll get back to you." And that's that, you know they're not calling.

When you start to drive home, you begin to feel sad and rejected. You wonder what happened and feel let down. What happened is that you declared something real, expected it to happen, and when it didn't, it began to erode your trust in yourself.

So how do you stop setting yourself up for disappointment? You have to shift your intentions to be really present with your interactions, your relationships, your projects, and with whatever is going on in your life. Really watch what is true in every moment. Don't cloud your experiences with wishful thinking. This will enable you to discern what is for you and what isn't. You will be able to stay detached from the outcome.

This is the key to moving out of disappointment and into grace: by practicing being present with what is and not projecting expectation. For example, let's take weight issues, which so many people deal with. If you tell yourself you're going to lose five pounds in the next two weeks and then only lose two pounds or none, you'll start to feel like a failure. But that's a setup. Why not set the intention that you will feel lighter, you will release weight, and you will see how your body cooperates to release as much weight as possible in the timeline set.

Trust that everything will work out to your advantage. That belief is one of the entry doors to grace. My mother raised me and my sister to trust life. Despite all the adversities and the many times things did not seem to be going her way—financial difficulties, my father's infidelities, having to work very hard to provide the things she wanted for her daughters—she would always say, "Something better will come our way." And it often did.

So when the things we wanted didn't work out, she would often say to us, "Obviously this was not for you." It happened over and over again. What a great attitude to have, to always assume that something better would come our way. The quickest way to get over feeling sorry for yourself is to give back—see the next chapter, "The Power of Service," for ways to switch your focus from yourself to others.

Remember that anything that doesn't work out wasn't meant for you. I love and use this positive statement often: "My heart is at peace knowing that what is meant for me will never miss me, and that what misses me was never meant for me." It shifts me into gratitude for what I have in my life. Try it. I have it framed on my desk. That statement shifts my attitude into trust. It is so great when we focus on the goodness that there is in our lives rather than what we don't have. That is a sure way to open the door to grace.

SUGGESTIONS FOR THIS WEEK

1. Write in your journal about your awareness of a situation in which you've experienced disappointment and start to discover the hidden blessing. If you assume that everything that happens is in your favor, what is the blessing in the situation? What are you being shown? What is the awareness that's to your benefit? Tell yourself, "This too is lifting me, this can teach me to be freer, more kind, more loving and accepting to myself."

2. Anticipate something that you're about to do and place the intention of less attachment to the outcome. Fill the situation with a sense of grace, of goodness, and project it without any preconceived ideas of how things should go. Start to experiment with the power of setting an intention rather than an expectation.

3. Experiment with yourself by observing what is. Don't place expectations on yourself, others, or situations. You can start to feel liberated, with a sense of freedom. Practice saying this positive statement to yourself often: In all my interactions, circumstances, and experiences, I practice being present, setting intentions, and letting go of expectations.

GUIDED MEDITATION

Find a comfortable position and allow yourself to relax. Shake your shoulders and release any tensions, anything you might be holding in your body, and take a deep breath and exhale with a sound, "Ahh." Be present in your body and in your heart. Bring into your awareness anything that might have caused you disappointment in your life; it could be recent, it could be in the past. Become aware of unmet expectations, what kinds of emotional discomfort they caused you, and what decisions you made about yourself when something didn't work out. Is there something you have told yourself you were going to commit to, but didn't? Or maybe something someone promised to you. So often in life, many things we want don't work out the way we would like them to. People don't meet our expectations. Even with ourselves, we often don't meet our own expectations. This is all part of the human condition. The added suffering is that we judge all of that. That judgment restricts our energy, our loving, and our ability to move forward.

So right now ask for the white light to fill you, surround you, and protect you, and imagine this beautiful, warm light embracing your body, emotions, and mind. Take this situation that has caused you disappointment and ask your wisdom and your highest self to show you the lesson that might be stored in this experience. What did this experience teach you about yourself? About others? About life? What is the lesson learned? If you made a decision about yourself or your life that does not support you in moving forward, can you allow yourself to forgive any judgments you may have made against yourself, or against another person? It could be "I forgive myself for judging myself for trusting too much," "I forgive someone else for not listening," "I forgive someone else for not taking enough time to review everything," or "I forgive myself for wanting things to turn out differently." In this forgiveness, experience a new sense of letting go. In this letting go, there is relaxation, a new surge of energy that's coming to you, a new enthusiasm, revitalizing you and renewing you to move forward from this experience. Knowing that you've become wiser and richer in your experience of this situation. Knowing that life is for you. Everything that happens is for your growth, your learning, and for you to know that you can access deeper, wiser parts of yourself.

In this deep acceptance right now, you start to experience a sense that you're not alone and you're anchored in your strength, in your clarity, and in your wisdom to move forward. Tuning into yourself, receive the guidance of what it is that you need to do next, what action you need to take. With new enthusiasm, you see yourself opening new doors that lead you to new vistas, being so supported by yourself, by others, and by your own spirit, you fill yourself with gratitude, you bless the past and release it. You now experience a newfound freedom, and how wonderful it is to let go of any burdens or disappointments. You return to your heart, your center, and your wholeness. When you're ready, you stretch your neck, shake your shoulders, wriggle your fingers and toes, take a deep breath, open your arms. Give yourself a big hug for your willingness to let go and be free; smile inside and out, radiating joy. When you're ready, open your eyes, have a sip of water to ground yourself, and you're ready to move on with your life.

40.

THE POWER OF
SERVICE

I slept and dreamt that life was joy. I awoke and saw that life was service. I acted and behold, service was joy.

—Rabindranath Tagore

When I was nine years old, my sister and I had taken on the cause of raising money for a little boys' orphanage. I would dance pieces that she had choreographed to raise money from our parents' friends. One time, we even decided to sell my parents' silverware to make more money—much to my parents' dismay! It worked—we brought the orphanage a radio, blankets, food. I've never forgotten how excited I felt doing something fun and creative to raise money for those in need.

It is such a gift to use your energy and natural talents to contribute to someone's life; it's truly the quickest way to feel like you are fulfilled and rich. One of my dearest friends is a ninety-year-old woman who struggles with a lot of health issues. All her life, she was a woman of service. She served my spiritual group and never made much money, but she says: "Agapi, I lack nothing. All of my needs are always met."

In today's world, there are thousands of causes and ways that we can serve others. You don't have to go to Africa to build schools or feed the homeless in your city or join the Peace Corps. These are all worthy causes and I commend you if you pursue them, but the consciousness of service is something that we can all practice and exercise in our lives every day. Service can show up in your relationships with your partner, children, siblings, parents, friends, coworkers, and even strangers. Just put your body, heart, and soul into being present and supporting others around you in any way you can. Being there can light up somebody's world. To do a little more in your own community, you can volunteer at your kids' school, mentor an at-risk child, coach a Little League team, or volunteer at a soup kitchen. Service is the quickest way to get us out of ourselves and find true fulfillment. In the art of giving, we find the art of living.

My mother had a very unique way of serving everyone she encountered in life. She always carried food with her and would offer nuts and treats to strangers. When we moved to Los Angeles, she would go to Whole Foods, buy a nice box of chocolates, and then hand it to the cashier. When she was in a taxi, she would open the divider and offer the driver an apple. The drivers were always stunned by this little Greek woman offering them sustenance. So often, the driver would come to our door to pay back the favor, offering us a kebab or fish and chips. My mother's theory was that life gives us life, and so giving back is really giving back to life. Feeding people was her unique way of serving.

After struggling to find work as a director, a friend of mine has made it his mission to teach senior citizens how to use computers, smartphones, the Internet, and social networks. He has created a community of people who teach technology to others. Seeing the senior citizens connect with their families on Facebook brings light into his life. This gives him so much energy to pursue his own dreams. Another friend of mine, completely frustrated with her corporate job and in deep pain from a hurtful relationship, decided to give it all up and join the Peace Corps. For two years, she served a community in Bulgaria. She ran a hip-hop group for teen girls and taught micro-entrepreneurship to minority women. After living without running water and electricity, she learned that "wants" and "needs" are different, and how to value what we are given. These two years changed her life forever. She returned healed, grateful, and ready for the next adventure. Now she's happily married and continues to love and serve the people around her. Another friend wanted to empower children through nutrition education. She started the organization Teaching Garden, which enables schools to develop organic gardens and supports them with a nutrition and fitness curriculum. With grassroots support, they are now planting gardens in a thousand schools. Seeing kids light up as they plant and pick their own vegetables brings her great joy.

Using your unique gifts to teach others skills that can add value to their lives and bring them joy brings joy right back to you. Find your own thing; open your mind. You would be surprised how something as simple as getting someone a cup of coffee can make his or her day. Service has no ego; it takes you outside yourself, bridges the separation, and connects us in our oneness.

SUGGESTIONS FOR THIS WEEK

1. Set an intention during your week that you will find opportunities to be of service. Watch out for them as they show up in your week. But also choose a particular situation that speaks to you. Pick something that will bring you and others joy. Write down in your journal how it affected your week just doing something for someone else.

2. If you're having a hard time finding something or you've been wanting to be of service but don't know where to start, check out www.volunteermatch.org, a great website for matching your gifts with a need.

3. Shift your mind-set this week to a "consciousness of service": I'm serving my children by making time to play with them; I'm serving my partner by romancing him or her; I'm serving my colleagues by providing a safe place for us to connect; I'm serving my friends by spending quality time with them; I'm serving strangers by smiling at them when we pass; I'm serving my environment by recycling. Just walk around with your intention to be of service.

41

ACCEPT WHEREVER YOU ARE RIGHT NOW

The place where you are right now, God circled on a map for you.

–Hafiz

In my forties, after pursuing my acting career and thinking about marriage, I shifted my outlook and path toward getting to know and fully expressing myself. It dawned on me that because I had shifted my focus, having children wouldn't be part of my life, and I had to face the reality that I was never going to be a mother. While this was not my dream, as a nurturing, loving woman, this awareness brought a sense of loss. I grieved. But once I surrendered to this fact, I realized that there was a deeper meaning for moving in this other direction; I was on a different journey. And then I saw the perfection of it all: Through my sister, I had two amazing nieces, with whom I am deeply connected. Giving them my motherly love made my heart full. In *accepting* my choice to not be married or have children, I felt free to create the possibilities to give my expression a full throttle outlet that brought me a lot of happiness. In surrendering and accepting this truth about myself, I was shown the wiser path. If I had been a full-blown wife and mother, like my mother had been, I never would have done Agapi and experienced my true fulfillment. I shifted from the "shoulds" to accepting what was right for me.

So often we judge where we are as wrong. This judgment distracts us from getting where we're meant to go. Take a look at your life and ask, "What am I judging about my life?" Maybe you're single and searching, but you feel a sense of incompleteness because you don't yet have the right partner. Maybe you're discontented with your work and you need to find something that calls to you. Maybe you have a creative idea for a startup or a book, but you feel overwhelmed by all the steps you need to take to achieve your goal. What if you stop resisting and accept where you are, and are honest with yourself so you can see the path intended for you?

This week, start by focusing on accepting exactly where you are and everything you feel about it. If you are tired and frustrated, be tired and frustrated. This is not a permanent state of being, just something you're moving through. If your children are driving you mad, and your husband is checked out, accept it and don't be bitter. If everyone around you is moving forward in their careers, accept it and know you're on your path. If your mother is driving you crazy, accept it and realize you can't control her. If the love of your life came and left, perhaps faster than you wanted, accept it and be grateful for this love. With this mind-set of acceptance, the grip of trying to control our lives releases. The people around us are not going to be the way we want them to be. They have their own codes of being, and when we accept them, with their differences, we will be at peace.

A friend of mine married a man who I thought was so wrong for her. It was very challenging to see her with him because I thought he should treat her differently. It took surrendering my judgments and opinions to accept that it was her choice and he was who he was. I said to myself, "Thank God, I didn't marry him!" I allowed my friend to go through her experience. In her own time, she left him, and our friendship survived because I had accepted that this was her journey.

As my spiritual teacher, John-Roger, so wisely pointed out: "Acceptance is not a passive state. Far from it. Acceptance is active because it requires you to be highly attentive. Acceptance has infinite subtleties and shadings. When you truly walk through the door of acceptance, you will experience joy and peace. You will be in the now. You will find yourself in your loving."

If you want to live in a different place, if you want a different job, a better relationship, a healthier lifestyle, a fit body, more friends, more fun and understanding and communication in your relationships, just start with what you have and accept it. Unconditional acceptance is the key to freedom. It is achieving a state of acceptance that gives you permission to be exactly where you are and go where you want to go.

Self-acceptance releases the pressure you put on yourself to be perfect. Accepting the circumstances of your life, accepting your so-called weaknesses, insecurities, your state of being just the *way you are* gives you breathing space. In this breathing space there is tremendous room for transformation and grace. In the gift of acceptance, you will see that the spirit resides where you are now, in everything, as is, and brings everything to perfect balance.

SUGGESTIONS FOR THIS WEEK

1. Throughout the next week, allow everything in your life to be the way it is. Accept it, not resisting, not trying to "fix" it.

Instead of contracting, take moments throughout your day where you consciously exhale. Keep a journal by your bedside and every night before you go to sleep record observations that have shown up during the day. How did you feel? Did you notice any shifts, sense of relief, or lack of tension?

2. As you look at yourself and your life and see things that you wish were different, observe the "shoulds" and judgments you might have made about your life. Find a place of forgiveness to let go of the judgments. Focus on the gifts you've been given. Make a list of them as if they are materials that have been given to you, and you are an artist starting work on a clean canvas. Know that like an artist, you have the ability to mix, blend, and erase.

3. In learning to fully accept everything about ourselves and our lives, we become like a gracious hostess who has room for everybody at her home but discerns who she will and won't invite again. In the simple act of accepting what is, we are free to choose where we are going to go next, what the next step is, and where we are going to place our focus. Keep your heart open to yourself no matter what. That's the ultimate key to transforming the conditions of your life. During your day, repeat this positive statement: "I unconditionally accept and embrace all the parts of myself and conditions of my life."

GUIDED MEDITATION

Find a comfortable position where you won't be interrupted for a little while. Come to a place of relaxation in yourself.

Relax your shoulders. Relax your neck. Shake your hands and feet and any tension you might be holding. Roll your shoulders a little bit. Begin letting go of things that bother you. Things that you cannot change in your life. Take a deep breath. As you exhale, exhale the tension and the resistance, the frustrations. Find a place inside of you that is patient, that is calm.

Allow your thoughts to pass you by like leaves in a river, giving them no energy, not wanting to change anything. Think of your life, the people around you, your work, things that you would like to go in a different way, faster. Outcomes you would like to see that might be taking longer than you want. Think of the people around you and how they aren't acting the way you would like them to. Maybe there are things that you try to control, or people you try to change, but they don't. People don't change, and circumstances don't seem to change. Start creating some distance between you and all the events of your life, as if you are watching scenes from a movie.

Between you and the scenes of your life, imagine a river of light that is coming straight from your heart, pouring out into every area of your life. Not wanting to change anything, this distance starts to bear a sweetness inside of you. You see the challenges, you see the different timing of you and your life. You see where there is wishful thinking that is not being executed. You see all the areas where you wish for different things to happen.

Inside of you, you say "It's okay, I'm okay, I'm okay that people are the way they are. I'm okay that things are taking a certain time. I'm okay that I am the way I am. I'm okay that I want things to be different. I'm okay that I feel the way I feel. I let go of the judgments against myself of feeling powerless, of feeling frustrated, of feeling sad. Any feelings that I have, I let go of judging them. I release myself from the pressure to change anything. I move into the vast field of acceptance. I move into a place of total neutrality about my life. I am more, way more than the events of my life. I am way more than the way things happen or don't happen. I am this river of calmness, of light, of peace, of strength, of wisdom. I allow this energy of deep acceptance to enter every cell of my body. I breathe it in and it brings me such happiness to know that I can relax and accept and that the love that is in me has the capacity to embrace everything. Everything I go through, everything other people go through, everything that happens, everything that does not happen. I make nothing wrong. It is watching the tapestry of life. Judging none of it. It is watching the game of chess with all the pieces moving, not moving, but I am the board where everything takes place. I am the board, where the game is played. And I'm steady. And I'm solid. And I'm happy. As I release this need to control, fear dissolves and love remains, wisdom guides, and my thoughts are uplifted to the realm of acceptance."

Now see that this quality of acceptance has filled your whole presence. You have allowed it in. Anchor it in your feet. Take your hands and place them on your belly. Place your hands on your heart. Touch the top of your head. Imagine beautiful hands are touching your shoulders, bringing a depth of relaxation that is so profound. Take a deep breath. Fill your lungs to capacity, and then gently exhale. Take another deep breath, and when you open your eyes, smile. You have been given the golden key of acceptance, knowing that you will know exactly what to do as you move forward in your life. Wriggle your hands, wriggle your feet. Turn your neck left and right. Take a deep breath and extend your arms. When you open your arms, open your energy. Give yourself a big hug. Take a sip of water to ground yourself. When you are ready, you might want to take your journal and jot down some thoughts that have become present about the field of acceptance in your life.

42.

MIX IT UP

It is a mistake for anyone to think he has lived too long in his old, unsatisfactory ways to make the great change. . . . Be teachable. That is the whole secret.

—Vernon Howard

Are you living on automatic? Are you at a point in your life where you feel stuck, bored, same old same old, and you're tired of your routine? You go to the gym and then to the office, you answer e-mails, go to meetings, have a coffee break with your work friend. You drive back home, make dinner, wash the dishes, take out the trash, catch up on the news, go to sleep, and repeat the cycle the next day. You are living on automatic and have built patterns that are safe and uncreative.

It's fine—more than fine, a privilege—to have a life with such order, with so many good things in it. Many of us seek out this kind of security. It gives us a sense that things aren't changing. It's comforting to live according to a pattern, but the truth is, everything in our world is constantly changing. A seed grows into a blossom, it blooms, then petals fall from the stem. This is the movement of life, nothing stays stagnant. Disrupting your patterns helps you shake up the status quo.

Maybe your routine is working against you, keeping you from

feeling that movement of the earth beneath your feet. Maybe you're missing opportunities, heartfelt moments, special experiences and connections. Maybe you're missing your aliveness and spontaneity—your joy.

If you are feeling comfortable but also a bit dull, if you're missing the juice of life, it's time to rekindle your curiosity and open up to try something new.

Let's start with your work life: after being in the office for hours, with meetings, e-mails, and deadlines, it is imperative that you get up and move: stretch or go for a walk around the block; look at how the leaves are changing on trees in the park, get some air! During your workday, when you're starting to feel stressed, why not stop and play a three-minute video of the cosmos; shift your perspective and fill yourself with the vastness of creation. After, you can go back to your e-mail and your deadline, but you'll feel how your body, mind, and spirit have shifted.

If you're eating the same easy, boring dinner several nights in a row, experiment with a new recipe. Move your furniture around! Go to a bookstore, browse in a genre you don't normally read, and buy something that catches your eye. Go shopping and try on a designer you can't currently afford—don't spend your money, just enjoy the experience, maybe snap a picture of yourself looking utterly fabulous in the dressing-room mirror. If you wear black every day, try orange. Use your left hand to write your grocery list—this actually helps develop a different part of your brain. Bake cookies (bring the extras to work the next day). Give your home an accent wall. Or ask a friend to help you redecorate. Just give yourself a new way to look at things, starting with the obvious: your home, your work, and yourself.

One time, I was jogging on the treadmill at the gym listening to disco, and a part of me felt completely uninspired. I thought,

"How boring is this? I don't want to do this." (I think we've all had this moment on the treadmill!) Instead of soldiering on, I stopped, left the gym, drove to the closest park I could find, put some music on, and started to exercise right there on the grass! I did my crunches while looking up at the sky and that simple action completely changed my perspective for the day.

Ask other people what helps them be creative and get inspired by their resourcefulness. My neighbor has her children bake when they get stressed about their homework; they forget their stress and refocus on something creative. When they return to their homework, they are much more lighthearted and energized, and better able to focus. Another friend runs a company, and every week she and a few colleagues take an improv class. She said it really gives them all such a laugh at themselves, and it completely shifts their seriousness to playfulness. What you lose by living on a schedule is your *laugh*. There's no room for a good time. That's a recipe for dullness and frustration. Find something or somebody that makes you laugh.

You can break the rules if they aren't working for you. It might make you feel vulnerable, uncomfortable, fearful. This is what happens outside your comfort zone. This is also where creativity happens. You are not a stagnant, unchanging being; you have edges and angles and bursts of energy that don't fit into your routine. Relish in your aliveness!

SUGGESTIONS FOR THIS WEEK

1. Write down in your journal what inspires you, who inspires you. Explore topics that intrigue you: science, art, languages, decor, politics, history, geography. If you're curious about something, explore it.

2. Memorize your favorite poem and romance yourself with these words. Share it with your friends. There's something so invigorating about reciting words that inspire you.

3. Continue to write in your journal and observe your daily life; see how you've been doing things. Observe and see if you're in a rut and ask yourself, "What would I like to do to experience more of my own aliveness?" Make a list of little things that can enrich and shift the monotony of your day and bring something new and bright into it. Then start doing these little things.

4. Become an adventurer and a collector of experiences within the life you have. Find friends, new and old, to enjoy in this new way of being.

43.

AWAKEN
YOUR JOY!

You carry all the ingredients to turn your existence into joy. Use them! Use them!

—Hafiz

As a child, I was always the life of the party. I wanted to make people happy and used every tool in my little pocket to bring joy: dancing, clowning, finding ways to make people around me laugh. Then, school came and joy went out the window. Then, life happened and I drew the curtain over the window. Seriously, who has time for joy when you are dealing with so much?

It wasn't until much later in my life, when I reconnected with my spirit and started to let go of limiting beliefs, that I let joy in. I let it spill over into my daily life. Oddly, I would often encounter people who felt threatened by this joy and tried to dampen it. When people are unhappy, they don't want joy around. They want to draw the curtain. But that's their problem, not yours. I had to learn not to censor my joy even if it made others uncomfortable. If people around you can't handle your joy, don't be around them. Find others who rejoice in your joy.

Now, that's not to say I'm always joyful, because I experience other emotions too. But in order to get back to my joy, I ask myself, "What's preoccupying me? What's making my heart unhappy? What are my concerns? What feelings do I need to address and let out to experience joy: is it sadness, anger, disappointment, fears, hurt feelings?" You can't just choose to feel joy. You need to express those other feelings first. If I numb myself to negative feelings, I'll numb myself to joy.

But I have some shortcuts to joy. Listening to music lifts my spirit, watching movies with someone I love relaxes me, working out to a great beat activates me, spending the day wandering without a to-do list frees me. All of these things bring me joy. My sister keeps pictures of her girls at various life stages near her—at home, in the office, and whenever she travels. They are her joy. I encourage you to find anything that delights you and keep that close to you.

Another joy trigger is to think of all the things that made you joyful as a child. For me, it was riding the Ferris wheel at the circus with my mom and sister; sleeping in a bunk bed on the train from Athens to Northern Greece; cutting pictures from magazines and making a collage on my bedroom walls. Later on, acting in plays and getting dressed up would bring me great joy. A friend who lives in Aspen triggers her joy by skiing; the moment she is on the slopes, she just beams! Another friend gets up at sunrise each morning to go surfing; communing with the ocean, the waves, and the whisper of the breeze is her practice of joy.

If you ever need a jolt of joy, listen to Beethoven's "Ode to Joy." There's a video on YouTube with a thousand voices in the choir. Honestly, if you're ever down, upset, depressed, or worried, put on your headphones and listen—it will change your brainwaves. Or maybe your joy comes from comedy. Larry David framed a rejection letter from one of the big networks that said, and I paraphrase, "Mr. David, *Seinfeld* will never amount to anything because it's about nothing." He keeps it in his bathroom. What's better than laughing about nothing, really? Don't you love it when people make you laugh about human nature and everyday life?

Between challenges with family and friends, workplace disagreements, health issues, money problems, and the news, we have our work cut out for us if we don't want to be swept away by negative energy. You must sustain the upward motion of a joyful attitude. You will definitely get a lot more done with way less stress if you keep focusing on the joy of you. Your day becomes easier when you set your intention to be grateful and know that the joy of your spirit will transform your life.

SUGGESTIONS FOR THIS WEEK

1. Take this week to make joy your priority. Build an inner environment of joy. Express your concerns, preoccupations, and emotions to guarantee that your joy will be welcome. Do whatever it takes to make sure nothing interferes with your joy. Build an inner connection to joy so that you have it at your fingertips. You can sing your favorite songs, you can play funny scenes in your mind, you can imagine your boss with fabulous pink bows if he's too serious. You don't have to tell anyone, just do it in your head. Delight yourself.

2. Make a list in your journal of the things that spark your joy. Be extremely creative and come up with at least twelve things (if

you have more, good for you!) that are very doable, and share your list with a friend. Keep yourself inspired.

3. Reaffirm that joy is not something you earn, it's inherent in your nature! When you're not living in your joy, you're denying yourself your birthright. Don't wait to earn joy.

4. Keep things around you that only give you joy: your clothes, your belongings, your favorite treats, your books, photographs, and other objects that mean something to you. Bring joy into everything you do. Believe me, your joy is there. It may be sleeping—don't wait for Prince Charming to wake it. Take it upon yourself to awaken your joy.

GUIDED MEDITATION

Find a comfortable position and settle in inside yourself. Take a deep breath, and as you exhale, release any tension, any preoccupations, and any worries. Settle into your heart and evoke an inner light that protects you, fills you, and surrounds you.

We are going to imagine some colors to help energize you and bring you into greater attunement with your inner consciousness. Take a deep breath and imagine the color red, and as you exhale, allow the color red to leave you. Now inhale while visualizing the beautiful color orange energizing you, refreshing you, and clearing up any cobwebs around your head.

Exhale and then inhale the beautiful color yellow. Let this

yellow bring you clarity and enthusiasm, piercing through anything inside you that feels disturbing.

Gently exhale, and then breathe in a bright emerald green. Place it around your eyes, and see a healing energy filling your body, restoring you to your optimal health.

Exhale this green, and as you inhale, imagine a beautiful blue that is bringing you a calmness and serenity; you can even visualize a beautiful blue lake in front of you making you feel ever so settled inside yourself. As you exhale this blue color, inhale a beautiful lavender that is attuning you to your wisdom, to your joy, bringing a presence of soulfulness to you. Exhale this lavender and imagine a white light coming from the bottom of your feet all the way up your spine to the top of your head and circling around you.

Take this white light, and all the other colors that you brought together, and imagine a huge rainbow that is forming an arc around you. This rainbow is showering you with a wonderful feeling of happiness and joy about your life.

See yourself in a big open field filled with sunflowers. See yourself walking freely with your feet touching the ground and with the breeze caressing your face as you feel the joy of your aliveness. It's like a bright spring day when everything is blooming and fragrant.

You are like a child, freely playing in this field. Bring friends if you wish, bring music that you love, and make this scene as happy as you like. Hear the birds singing. Smell the fragrances of joy.

Experience yourself as a person who is finding joy in everything you do. Bring that feeling of joy and infuse your life with it. Your essence, and who you are in spirit, is naturally filled with joy. See yourself waking up in the morning, setting an intention that your joy will be present through-out your day. Keep rekindling your joy throughout your day, remembering that joy is who you are.

Take a deep breath and exhale slowly, and bring your-self present, keeping this feeling of joy alive. Keep anything that awakens that joy in you vivid in your imagination. Take a deep breath, exhale, and imagine this beautiful big rain-bow all around you, embracing you, surrounding you. Ex-hale with a joyful sound, "Ahh."

Now then, let's take one more deep breath and open your arms and exhale with another joyful sound, "Ahh." You are ready to have a day filled with joy.

44.

THE POWER
OF AN
OPEN HEART

If you wish to be loved, love!

—Seneca

Have you ever met someone who makes you feel warm and up-lifted? Who touches your heart? You probably never wanted to leave their side. Growing up in Greece, I was surrounded by heartwarming people like this; they were physically, emotionally, and verbally affectionate. Greeks have an innate ability to express themselves from a heartfelt place. From serving you a meal to opening their homes to strangers, there is a caring that goes beyond the call of duty. There is nothing more wonderful than experiencing the warmth of a connected and open heart. What a world it would be if we all lived and acted from that caring, loving place. However, our human tendency to criticize and judge cuts off our heartfelt energy toward ourselves and each other.

We shut off our hearts when we are hurt. We are all afraid to show our real self because we think we are alone in our vulnerability. When I saw my parents not being loving to each other and closing their hearts as they went through a divorce, I was hurt, and I started to close myself off from the world. Witnessing their divorce impacted the way I filtered love and set a pattern of looking for outside validation and feeling pain when that validation didn't come. I felt hurt when I didn't get the acting parts I wanted, I felt hurt when relationships didn't work out, I felt hurt when my dreams and expectations weren't being met. My heart staying open was always dependent on the outside outcome, and my self-love was very conditional: if I got what I wanted, I was elated; if I didn't, I shut down.

Ironically, my name, Agapi, means "unconditional love" in Greek, and that is what life was teaching me—the importance of unconditional love. As I became aware of my undermining pattern of loving myself only conditionally, I had to ask myself, "Why am I giving so much importance to these outer results? And why is my self-love so conditional?" That's definitely not a way to live and be happy. Trust me! So I explored the root of this pattern and found out how and when it started. Then I embarked on a journey of forgiveness. I forgave my parents for the pain their separation caused, and this helped to untie the knots that were binding my heart.

I chose to prioritize my creativity over my expectations of a successful career. I stopped thinking about finding "the one" and learned to enjoy whoever I was spending time with. It was a journey from blame and entitlement to gratitude; from feeling like a victim to empowerment. Ultimately, instead of feeling sorry for myself, I started to appreciate who I was and not take myself for granted. From this place of acceptance, my heart opened up. I let out that part of myself that's warm and exuberantly affectionate—I found my ability to connect with others and I saw how other people responded, and that filled me with joy. I realized that everybody is longing for that connection, but they are waiting for the other person to open up first because they don't want to be rejected. I made a conscious choice to take the lead and not wait for the other person. Everywhere I went, I had countless heart-felt encounters.

If you find yourself feeling stuck, down, anxious, bitter, or pessimistic, I guarantee that your heart is closed at that very moment. You probably have critical judgments of yourself, others, and life, and you feel isolated. From here, you have a choice. You don't have to stay in this place. Know that at that moment, you are longing for connection with yourself. Ask yourself, "Why am I withdrawing my self-love?" Listen for the response. Is it something current or old? Be honest and allow yourself to be vulnerable, because it is through that vulnerability that our hearts soften. You might need to cry because something is releasing. You might need to write down all the pent-up feelings that have been stored under judgments and criticism. Just know that under all of that weight, your heart is longing to open and be given permission to express all of your pain, hurts, and hopes, and ultimately love. Don't live in the separation between you and your heart, it's not a good way to live. Do whatever it takes to heal the separation.

I learned this lesson after I didn't get a part in a Greek play I'd auditioned for. I found myself on a New York City bus feeling utterly miserable. I sat down next to a woman, and for some reason, we spontaneously connected. We started chatting, and I discovered that she was a former actress herself. One thing led to another, and I ended up performing one of my favorite monologues from the play *Saint Joan* by George Bernard Shaw, just for her, right there on the bus! My portrayal of Joan touched her deeply. She reached out, held my hand, and said, "My dear girl, you are so talented, why wait for anyone to hire you? Go do your own thing."

That comment from a woman on a bus whom I would never see again changed the course of my life. I found freedom when I shared my heart unconditionally and performed for her. From that moment on, I took my life into my own hands. I stopped waiting for other people to give me permission to do anything. The spark that was ignited on the bus led me to find my own way, to express my creativity in forms I had never imagined. No longer was I waiting for the validation of a casting director. I experienced how rich our lives can be in sharing our gifts unconditionally with other human beings.

That was my liberation: freely sharing my joy. What is yours? It is imperative that you find the sweetness of your heart, what opens it up, what releases and expresses it. I know one thing for sure: our hearts thrive in giving, caring, and sharing without end or agenda.

Bring your heart with you, everywhere you go. Don't leave it behind when you go out into the world. So many times people go to work with walls around their heart, thinking, "I've got to be efficient and productive and there's no room for joy." But haven't you found that you get far more accomplished when your heart is engaged? Once your heart is healed and open, it grows by being shared. This is not about wearing your heart on your sleeve; that expression is about your emotional heart, the part of you that gets hurt. This is about being centered in your spiritual heart and sharing it from a discerning, strong, and truthful place. My experience is that when we are anchored in truth, our hearts are mighty. That's when we are more effective and more productive, and experience more aliveness because we have a lot more energy to cut through walls. This openness spontaneously engages other people and warms up our hearts.

The guided meditation in this chapter will help you become

anchored and mighty in the center of your heart, like the eye in a hurricane. Once you have access to that, the world is yours. So don't miss the moment. You're worth it.

SUGGESTIONS FOR THIS WEEK

1. This week, make loving your intention. Look at the areas in your life where you judge and shut off your loving. Look at the areas where things happen that upset you. Do these things shut off your heart? Can you give yourself a break and suspend judgment of yourself or of other people? Write down what comes up.

2. Every day, throughout your day, take little moments to place your hand on your heart—focus inward, pulling energy and love to yourself—remembering who you are beyond your feelings, mind, personality, and circumstances. Say over and over again, "I love you no matter what. I love you no matter what. I love you no matter what." Let it sink in until it moves you to peace.

3. Have random moments of heartfelt connection. When you interact with people, look at them with the eyes of love and watch how your heart moves you to do or say things that lift people.

GUIDED MEDITATION

Find a comfortable position and take a few moments to center in your heart. This can be done anytime throughout your day, it can even be done at work, in a public place, or at your home. We are going to access the power of your heart.

Take a deep breath and relax into your heart. Take another deep breath and slowly exhale. Allow your whole energy to fill your heart; not just your physical heart, but your emotional and your spiritual heart. If you would like, you can take both your hands and gently place them on your heart. As you take your next breath, allow your heart to open. Imagine a beautiful rose, a full, in-bloom rose, any color you want in the center of your heart. Every time you take a breath, a petal opens. You have moved all your stress from your mind and emotions and returned to the clarity of your heart.

Think of things that awaken your love. Is it your child? A friend? A family member? Your partner? Your pet? Or perhaps it is a photograph of a sunrise or sunset. Bring them present to you right now. Let the sweetness of that thought fill you up and tell yourself, "This is love. This love lives inside of me." If you notice any pain, disappointments, separation, anxiety, or grief, acknowledge them. Notice the energy of your heart awakening and embracing all of your sadness and gently and lovingly transmuting any energies that you don't need. Thoughts of worry, of future outcomes, are transformed right now in the presence of the power of your heart. Repeat this statement in your mind: "I am safe to keep my heart open. Protected in the knowing of my heart. I listen to my heart. I listen to the quiet whisper that my heart tells me. I listen to its wisdom, tenderness, kindness, and compassion, and I respond to the calling of my heart."

Take that love and amplify it right now. Let yourself be embraced by it. Breathe it into your lungs, all the way.

Let the love rise up through your body and comfort you. If there are tears that come, let them come. It's the willingness to surrender to the love of who you are that ultimately will open your heart. The rose in your heart has opened its petals and released its fragrance. Now, from that centered place, contained and yet expanded, send love out like beams of sunlight, out into your family, into your work, into your home, and into every area of your life. This ray of sun will connect you within and thread your life with love. Even send love to the situations that disturb you, and see how they change. This is you. This love is who you are.

Return to this place often. It's the home of your heart; live in it. It has wisdom, direction, and guidance for you. Fill it with sunlight. You have the choice to come back to the home of your heart. When the world pulls you, your heart is your sanctuary.

Take a deep breath, raise your arms and extend them out, taking in all of this energy and give yourself a big hug. Tilt your head to the left and to the right. Let your heart energy move through you. Take a deep breath and exhale with a sigh . . . be happy. You know your heart. It's so simple. It's your very breath. Smile. Drink a sip of water. Write down something that connected you back to you. When you stand, feel your heart throughout your body. When you go out into the world, know that you are protected and surrounded by that love. Let it radiate out. You're going to have an amazing day.

45.

LOVING YOURSELF

The greatest thing in the world is to know how to belong to oneself.

—Michel de Montaigne

"How do I love myself?"

This is one of the most common questions I am asked at my teaching seminars. We all know—in our minds—that in order to experience a happy and fulfilled life, we must first have love and compassion for ourselves.

But gosh darn it, why is it so hard to do?

All the spiritual teachings encourage us to look inside and find that self-love. We go on quests and journeys because we yearn to know our "self" and our belovedness. There are hundreds of affirmations looming before us that say, "I love and accept myself unconditionally. I am a divine being. I am enough. I have all the resources I need." But, if you are like me, I can say these affirmations until the cows come home and still not feel a thing! "Fake it till you make it" doesn't really work, either. And I'm sorry to say, neither does retail therapy!

Truly loving yourself means that you must be willing to "go

there." And "there" is *the most vulnerable, unglamorous, raw part of you.*

Let's take a look at Raymond Carver's wonderful poem "Late Fragment":

And did you get what
you wanted from this life, even so?
I did.

And what did you want?
To call myself beloved, to feel myself
beloved on the earth.

We all desire the same thing: to be seen, cherished, and loved as we are. We spend so much of our lives yearning for a sense of belonging and connection at the deepest level. We seek to find that one person who will love us unconditionally so that we will finally know that we are truly beloved. But this is a backward approach! Because what if that person isn't out there? What if we don't find that person or we find them and they leave us? Or change toward us? Then what?

When you don't know how to nurture and take care of yourself—how to be in a healthy, loving, intimate relationship with yourself—you can start to feel exiled, neglected, undernurtured, unattended, and ignored. You try to fill this void created by self-neglect by looking outside yourself, hoping that others can fill up this hole.

A few years ago, at a seminar with my spiritual teacher, I shared that I was searching for happiness and a deeper sense of connection. He looked at me and in a matter-of-fact way said, "You take the sequins from the left side of your dress and put them on the right, thinking that things will be different. But they won't change because you are avoiding the primary relationship with yourself." He meant that I was looking to other relationships, work, friendships to find meaning when really I needed to spend time with Agapi and get to a place of feeling comfortable with myself. I heard him loud and clear; he was right, but I didn't know how to *not* do that anymore.

At that period of my life, I was feeling excruciatingly lonesome and insecure, with little sense of self, and a lack of direction. I was in pain. I couldn't face the pain, so I had found hundreds of ways to distract and avoid myself. It takes a lot of courage and vulnerability to tell yourself, "I'm in pain. I feel hurt, lost, disconnected, insecure." That open communication is the most loving thing we can do to and for ourselves—to go to those places that hurt, are insecure, and are unexplored. My habit was always to go to another person and take care of him or her. In comforting someone else, I comforted myself. Or I would plunge into a romantic relationship to find "meaning." But wouldn't you know it, in the dynamic of a relationship, all of those unresolved emotions that I was trying to avoid would surface.

Through my spiritual practices, I learned two great keys to loving myself: forgiveness and self-appreciation. One day, when a romantic relationship was no longer working for me and I was in a lot of pain because this person was not loving and supporting me the way I wanted to be cared for, I got so sick and tired of my neediness that I sat on my bed and prayed. My prayer turned into a stream of uninterrupted forgiveness. It went something like this:

I forgive myself for judging myself for feeling needy. I forgive myself for judging my partner for causing me pain. I forgive myself for judging myself for causing myself pain because this person doesn't love me the way I want to be loved. I forgive myself for judging myself for believing that unless I am loved by another, I am not whole and complete.

I went on and on, and then moved into forgiveness about the judgments of not being successful "enough."

I forgive myself for judging myself for not being more successful. I forgive myself for judging myself for feeling I should be recognized as an actress. I forgive myself for judging myself for feeling frustrated that my projects are taking so long to manifest. I forgive myself for judging myself for not knowing all the answers.

And on and on.

Every time I made a forgiveness statement, I actually went there—to the very core of my being—and touched the girl who was struggling with everything. And I cried. I let her cry, for my struggles and my loneliness, for feeling that life isn't fair, for feeling helpless, for wanting to be happy but not knowing how to get there. With this surrender, the spirit in me was beginning to open, the light in me was beginning to glow in my closed places, and I was opening my heart to myself.

I got to the bottom of the barrel and saw that a lot of my pain and feelings of disconnectedness were being caused by my self-judgments, by feeling that things should be different. But it wasn't a bottomless pit because there was an end to these judgments. *There was a bottom and it was solid.* I had to fill the barrel with my own self-appreciation, compassion, and acceptance in order to bring in the light. That's when I started to realize that loving myself started with the fundamental belief that I was going to be there for myself, *no matter what.*

I started making self-appreciating statements in my mind: I appreciate myself for being willing to let go of things that don't work for me; I appreciate myself for the courage to support myself; I appreciate myself for my kindness and thoughtfulness; I appreciate myself for the strength that it takes to follow a spiritual path; I appreciate myself for being willing to examine the areas of my life that are painful; I appreciate myself for being fun and spontaneous; I appreciate myself for my warmth; I appreciate myself for being a good daughter and sister; I appreciate myself for being able to overcome rejections and keep seeking my purpose; I appreciate myself for going to yoga; I appreciate myself for making time to share authentically with my friends.

I went on and on.

And from my willingness to listen to the direction my teacher had given me, there was a change. I let go of holding on so tight to how I thought my life should be. My willingness to be naked to my own self moved me to a place where I felt I was being held by the loving presence within me. I started to focus more on the gratitude, and less on the lack.

As life went on, things kept happening that triggered self-judgments. It took me time to find the correct direction in my life, to build a path that felt more solid and connected. That practice of "I forgive myself for judging myself . . ." bridged the gap from disappointments, rejections, comparisons, and jealousies to a place of "I appreciate myself . . ."—a place of contentment, peace, and self-love. I started to feel more nurtured and secure.

When I dare to turn my eyes inward, to my goodness and beauty and the loving person that I am, and give that gift to myself, it is absolutely heavenly. When I tend to myself in small ways and make the right choices to support myself daily—how I eat, how I exercise, how I listen to myself, who I work with, how I take care of my environment—and when I am willing to partner with myself and say, "We are in it together. Let me help you with this," I always find my way back to self-loving. Open self-communication is key to staying in tune with yourself and finding that happy place. Practice ultimate self-care and constant appreciation: *treat yourself like someone you dearly love* and see how everything in your heart will start to soften and open a space for love to come in.

When you have prepared a place for love to come in, your spirit will meet you there. Reading poetry connects me to the spirit within. Before going to bed, I read Rumi, Hafiz, Kabir—these mystic poets who had such a profound union with the divine spirit open me up to my own inner spirit, tapping into that place that is love, unconditional love. No expectations, no "shoulds," no pressure, just deep acceptance of what is. It's like having an Inner Lover that you walk hand in hand with throughout your life, constantly romancing you. I have felt this Inner Lover many times. Have you ever sat by a tree in a relaxed moment, on the grass, gazing into the horizon, and felt a soft breeze caress your body, and suddenly you feel not only at peace, but also a little euphoric? That's the closest thing I can describe to experiencing the Inner Lover.

This experience is available to all of us, regardless of our conditions. It just takes a willingness on our part to open up to it . . . even in the middle of washing dishes! My mother used to experience joy and union with her spirit when she would spontaneously go to the ocean and feed the seagulls. I feel it when I listen to Mozart's piano sonatas. What opens you up and softens your heart? Go there . . . often. When our hearts open and soften, we start to feel connected to other people's hearts and can experience our oneness.

GUIDED MEDITATION

Find a comfortable position in a quiet space where you won't be interrupted. Settle in inside yourself. Let go of any tensions in your mind, in your emotions, let go of any worries that you might be carrying in your shoulders. Shake your shoulders a little bit. Turn your neck from left to right. Relax your arms and legs. Allow yourself the gift of a deeper relaxation.

Let the stress melt away. Imagine a beautiful soft warm white light embracing you from the top of your head all the way down to your feet, protecting you and making you feel very safe. Focus on your heart. Take a deep breath and exhale. Take another deep breath and slowly exhale. Fill your lungs, your heart, and your whole body with an energy of love. Wherever you can find a loving space inside of you, just bring it into yourself, to your heart.

Take a little journey into your daily life over the course of the years. Start to see the core places where you are holding loving back from yourself. Look at situations and interactions with people, and see yourself throughout your day, how you end your day as you are about to go to sleep. Is there a place inside of you that could use more loving and more appreciation? Is there a place inside of you where you are judging yourself because you think you should be different? Where you feel you are lacking in something? Are there places where you are taking yourself for granted? Ask yourself if there is something you can let go of right now. Is there something you might be able to forgive? Complete this sentence with what you need to forgive: "I forgive myself for judging myself for thinking _____. Any feelings, any thoughts, any hurts? What if you knew that you were perfect, lovable, worthy, and beautiful just the way you are? Unique, one of a kind. In the whole universe, there is no one like you. What if you really knew that there is nothing wrong with you? You are a work of art in progress. What if you were to open yourself and say thank you to yourself: "Thank you for being who you are"? What if you opened up your heart so deeply, so wide, and you loved you? You just loved you just as you are right now.

Listen to yourself. Ask your heart if there is something you need to hear to know that you are loved. Is there something you need to let go of to know you are loved? Are there any conditions you put there? "I will love myself when . . ." "I would love myself if only I had . . ." "I would love myself if so-and-so loved me." What if you could love yourself without any of that now and know that you are beloved? Turn your focus inward and open up the locked places of your loving. Fill yourself with compassion, with self-appreciation, and know that right now you are receiving the love of who you are.

Take your right hand and place it on your belly, take your left hand and place it on your heart. Breathe in a beautiful light and tell yourself, every day my life gets better and better. Every day, I learn a little more how to love myself. My sense of worth is not measured by my accomplishments, my achievements, or how other people react to me. I feel warm and loving toward myself, for I am worth my own loving and I'm perfect in my essence. I let go of anything I've been holding against myself. I do the best I can with what I know in the circumstances. I forgive my mistakes, I forgive other people's mistakes toward me, and I'm free.

I stand tall, giving no authority to anyone else but standing in my own truth. I face everyone with a friendly and open countenance. I listen to my inner guidance, I follow it, and I stay in tune with myself. I take good care of myself, I make myself a priority, and I ask for what it is I want. I allow myself to receive, to be opened, and to ask. I give myself permission to live, to laugh, and to love in my fullest capacity.

Take a deep breath, exhale slowly as you open your arms, extend that big light all around you and take it in and know that you are loved and you are there for yourself, and you dare to love yourself.

See yourself smiling from the inside out. Take a deep breath, exhale with a sound, "Ahh." And when you are ready, in this new energy of loving yourself, open your eyes. Take a sip of water, and when you stand, stand ten feet tall.

46

FROM STRUGGLE TO GRACE

Grace is not hard. Grace is not something you go after as much as it is something you allow. You just let it become. You may want it to come like thunder, lightning, or a big train so you know it is there—you know, with lots of noise and drama. It comes in naturally, however, like breathing, and you may not even know it is happening.

—John-Roger

After I graduated from drama school in London, I was hired to act in a movie filming in Los Angeles. For two months, I was filled with hope and anticipation about what was about to happen. Then, suddenly, the financing of the movie fell through. I was free to return to London. Like the movie, my dream had fallen through. But I drew on my courage and made the choice to stay in L.A. and face the unknown. To me, the unknown just looked like empty space. Money was tight, family was far away, I didn't have any faith or a higher power to look to. I felt displaced and lost.

I started to explore, looking for meaning. I found connection in the daily practice of yoga. I started to read spiritual books, including *The Autobiography of a Yogi* by Paramahansa Yogananda, a book my mother had introduced to me when I was a teenager.

As I immersed myself in the wisdom and journey of this amazing man, something extraordinary started to happen. I started to awaken, remembering that there was another reality beyond Hollywood. I wasn't just this Greek girl seeking a career in film, I had a soul and was a part of a much larger whole. One night, I fell asleep reading the book and was awakened the next morning by the early sunlight pouring through my window. Simultaneously, an inner light reignited and I was illuminated from within. I felt like I had pierced the heavy ceiling of this world and made a little hole where the light could come down to me and fill me.

I fell to my knees and started to cry, saying, "Father, Father, Father, I know that I am a child of God." I don't even know where these words came from, but it was a visceral, heartfelt experience filled with a deep knowledge that I was not alone, but absolutely connected to the divine source. I knew this was grace.

In that moment, something profound had opened up in me and I knew my life was about to change. I felt elated, and I wanted to go out into the street shouting, "Eureka, I've got it! I'm not alone, I belong, I am loved." But I didn't. Instead, I called a friend to have lunch and as I sat with her, I wondered how to share this profound experience—and then as I watched her, I saw her with new eyes and found a new appreciation for her aliveness and soul. I never gave her the details of my morning experience, but something had shifted in me. At the end of lunch, she asked me, "You're glowing. Did you get a part?" I smiled and knew that my world had changed. Everything around me started to take on a new color, texture, and meaning. I felt alive, grounded, and connected.

I still didn't know what my next move would be, but now I had a source to ask. So I prayed and said, "Dear God, can you help me find a teacher in this path? I need a teacher to help guide me back home." Before long, I met an extraordinary teacher named John-Roger at the spiritual center, Prana, in Los Angeles. The first time I met him, he gave me a big hug and said, "Welcome home, beloved." I never looked back. He became my spiritual teacher and was invaluable in teaching me how to integrate the spiritual and material worlds and find the teacher within.

Life went on with all its challenges, but I could always feel the warmth of my inner light. That light would grow in me and around me as I sought it, softening life's struggles and releasing the inner knots. The more I trusted it and was willing to "let it in," the more grace-filled my life became. So even in the middle of adversity and challenges, and moments of disconnect, I chose to return to that place that comforted me, never judged me, never demanded but deeply loved and accepted me. This place of love was the seat of my soul.

Grace is defined as "free and unmerited favor from God." To me, that means grace is like my very own breath. It's always there. It flows through me. Like our breath, grace is effortless, but we don't know it's there until we decide to focus on it. We are wired as human beings to wear our struggles like badges of honor; we feel we have to prove ourselves good and worthy in order to receive this extraordinary gift of grace. But this is like saying, "I have to earn each breath." You don't. It's given freely.

Now, imagine a life without the weight of struggle. You can experience that by changing your perception of how you relate to the issues in your life. As Shakespeare wrote, "There is nothing good or bad but thinking makes it so." Isn't it ironic how in the struggle, we find meaning? We get addicted to the conflict. We allow it to define us, which limits us. Thinking this way is erroneous. Let go of the attachment to your struggle and shift from judging yourself and the circumstances you are in to accepting where you are right now. Something bigger is going on in your life, and although that's not felt or seen, trust that it is cradling you and it will carry you through. In this state, you will experience the fullness of grace.

Accepting your lot in life is a personal journey. What keeps you from acceptance is self-imposed pressure, comparison, and a demand that things should be different. When you surrender to your reality, grace flows through your life. The struggle ceases. Everything feels all right. You have inner security. When you shift into grace, miraculously, things start to change right in front of you. Things fall into place: deadlines are met, connections are made, forgiveness reigns, confidence grows, trust abounds, love is present, joy awakens. In giving up the struggle, you become a kinder, gentler, calmer, happier person, ushered forward by grace.

GUIDED MEDITATION

Find a comfortable position where you won't be interrupted for a few moments and start to attune to your own inhalation and exhalation. Slow down your breath and observe the rising and falling of your breath. Ask for an inner light to fill you, protect you, and surround you. Take in this light that's helping you relax, let go, and release any tensions and worries of your life. We are going to move into a deeper receptivity to the spirit that lives in us, and the spirit that sustains you and all things. Just allow yourself this moment to come into a reverence for your own life. Take a look at your life and see where your focus is for most of your day. Is your focus mostly on your problems? On your to-do list? On thinking that things will not work out for the best? Is your focus on worrying? So often we are so programmed to think about the worst and focus on the problems, rather than the solutions. Just for this moment, allow yourself to shift your focus, knowing that the spirit of life that sustains you can spill over to every aspect of your life.

Take a situation now where you feel you are struggling. Isn't struggle a tightening up, a resistance—making things wrong, not giving yourself breathing space? What if the struggle were replaced by a sense of grace? Let's imagine for this moment that this is so. Imagine where there is tightness in your body, in your emotions, in your thoughts. What makes you tight? Is it the judgment? Is it a resistance to what is? Is it a holding back of your own breath? Take a deep breath and breathe into that tightness, and as you breathe, imagine that there are pathways where you have placed restrictions and imagine that the road is clearing. Where there have been thoughts of restriction and constriction, now it's opening up. The path is opening, it's expanding, and you can see clearly ahead of you on the road. Just imagine and visualize a light that is clearing up any cobwebs, any confusion, and any fear. This light brings you such calmness and such security, and you are letting it in, infusing every aspect of your life, and especially this situation that you have been struggling with. You have nothing to do but give it over to this light. You might want to say to yourself, "I bring this situation to the light and surrender it. I go free. I surround it with light, release it and let it go. My struggle dissolves, diminishes, and disappears, and in its place, I see the power of grace, which is as simple as letting it go and trusting that the source of what gives me life, is also helping me in this area."

Just right now, breathe that new energy in: an energy of calmness, expansion, clarity, of turning your focus back to knowing that all things are well. Let this grace just take over. Allow it to take over. Take your hands and place one on your belly and the other on your heart. Breathe into your heart, belly, back, and lungs and fill your whole self with this grace. Let everything inside of you soften. Let this light illuminate the areas that have been harsh and tight. Stay there for a few moments. Just bathe in it. When you're ready, shake your shoulders, wriggle your fingers and toes, take your arms and open them wide with a big sigh. Take one more deep breath, lift your arms in a circling motion and exhale with another sigh . . . "Ahh." Now you're ready to go on to the next thing in your life, filled with a feeling of grace.

47.

GOD IS YOUR PARTNER

I'll never forget the day that I chose to make God my partner in every aspect of my life. It was a very distinct moment. But before I tell you about that, let me just explain what I mean by God.

I was listening to the poet Mark Nepo speaking to a group, and he asked them if they believed in something larger than themselves. Everyone raised their hands. And he said, "Well then, you're all mystics." To me, that's what God really is: it's something that is larger than ourselves.

Universal love, the cosmos, divine intelligence, the big blob in the sky, whatever you call it, it's the very thing that moves our bodies and makes us breathe—that power that is incomprehensible and impossible to define, or to capture in the three-letter word *God*. This awesome, inexplicable presence is what I'm talking about.

In the chapter "Finding Grace in Disappointment," I talked about my experience developing a biopic on the Greek singer Maria Callas. We had hired a very well-established international director to make the movie with us, and I had partnered with an affluent Greek to finance it. Together, we went through the process of mounting a production: holding endless meetings, interviewing writers, developing a script, and so on. We were especially shocked when our famous director ended up, for lack of a better word, screwing us over. He took the money, kept us waiting, and made his own movie about Maria Callas. After my disappointment I decided to move on and secured the interest of a major Hollywood studio. However, my extremely stubborn partner started demanding to have his way in the process of firming up a deal with the studio. When the studio almost cut its ties with us because of his stubbornness, I called him and said, "We are either going to comply with their terms together, or I'm going to proceed on my own." He replied, "You can't do that because I'm your partner." Now remember, he was the one with all the money, the lawyers, the one who wrote the checks. It was scary to think of letting him go.

I don't know what prompted this gutsy response in me, but I heard myself say to him, "Yes, but I have a bigger partner: God. And He will help me make it on my own!" I remember making this declaration with absolute certainty. In that moment I was endowed with a monumental strength that produced chills up and down my spine. It felt as if my very life force and spirit were backing me. So, I let him go and moved forward on my own.

Right after that call, I took a yellow pad and a big red marker and wrote, "God Is My Partner." I framed it and hung it on my office door so that it was the first thing I saw in the morning. These four words became my mantra and made me feel very solid because I had released the fear that I was alone. The movie never materialized, but that hardly matters compared to what I gained from this experience: the firm knowledge that God is my partner in everything I do.

This lesson has guided me at different stages of my life:

moving from Los Angeles to New York, letting go of a dead-end relationship, writing my first book, living on my own, asking for help from different people, finding the right apartment on my budget, making new friends, attending events and functions as a single woman—in things both large and small. It has helped me build an unshakable trust in myself. Whenever I wavered or felt insecure or terrified of the unknown, I continued to affirm, "God is my partner . . . God is my partner" until the very cells within me began to vibrate with this belief. I became a witness to the small miracles around me that enriched my daily life.

I have a tribe of girlfriends who have also adopted this belief. We often remind each other of it whenever we are worried, disappointed, or waver from this belief. When they ask me, "Who is your partner?" I reply, "God," and a lightbulb switches on in my brain.

I also practice this belief whenever I feel overwhelmed about a new venture: writing a new book, conducting seminars abroad, developing a new creative idea. I trust my inner wisdom to slow me down and lighten the load, focusing once again on taking care of myself by breathing deeply, letting go, getting better sleep, eating healthfully, laughing, having a good time, relinquishing perfection, lightening up, and trusting that things will get done easier that way. I think that experiencing God in this way has allowed me to open my heart and become more loving and accepting of myself and others.

SUGGESTIONS FOR THIS WEEK

1. Start this week by focusing on this notion: What would you be like if you made the statement "God is my partner" a reality in your life?

2. Fill yourself with a sense of awe that you've been given your breath. Allow your mind to quiet while you become present in the force that is moving through you, through your blood, and the extraordinary brilliance of how your body functions. This complex organism that digests, breathes, pumps blood, and loves is a miraculous, extraordinary, and complete gift, so allow yourself to be in awe and partner with that force in your life.

3. When we affirm something so powerful and monumental that it can totally shift our life, it's inevitable that doubt will come up. This can be a thought that runs through our head saying, "Who do you think you are, calling God your partner?" The saboteur in us, who doesn't want us to have what we want, will try to bring us down. If your first attempt fails, don't lose heart or hear the negative thinking, but keep affirming it, staying the course, and knowing that God is indeed your partner. Repeat this positive statement: "The force of life that moves in me is helping me in every aspect of my life because God is my part-ner. I give myself permission to know this as a fact and claim it for myself."

GUIDED MEDITATION

Come into a comfortable position. Start to breathe in and out very slowly. Relax into your own breath and observe the inhalation and exhalation of your breath. Start to at-tune to yourself, letting go of the tensions of your day, the worries and the preoccupations. Relax your shoulders. Take another deep breath and fill yourself with the power and gift of your breath. We're going to go through some colors to get you more attuned to your own self. The color red—imagine the color red infusing you and energizing you. Exhale the red and breathe in the color orange—giving you new vitality. Exhale the color orange and breathe in the color yellow—giving you clarity, inspiration, and a sense of strength. Breathe out the color yellow and breathe in the color green—a beautiful, healing green that takes care of every aspect of your health and your energy for the day—and filling your whole body with a soothing emerald green. As you exhale the green, just breathe in a beautiful blue—this blue brings you calmness, serenity and a sense of peace. As you exhale the blue, breathe in a beautiful, lavender purple that's taking you deeper into yourself, relaxing you, making you feel safe, secure, and protected. Breathe out the purple and breathe in a beautiful white light. This white light that infuses you from the top of your head to the bottoms of your feet, up and down, brings you such calmness and clears out any cobwebs or distractions in your mind that have been disturbing your clarity of purpose and your ability to be fully present.

Start to connect with a presence and power that is larger than you; the energy that is breathing you, that is giving you your life force, the universal energy that makes everything move, and function beyond your understanding. Just for a moment, take in the miracle of life that you are. As you breathe it in, that power that is with you, allow yourself to be receptive and feel totally supported by this energy. If you look at your life, you will get a sense that there is a higher purpose and a higher energy that is guiding everything. Attune yourself to that, allow yourself to receive that energy and light right now. As you imagine your day, your life, and all the things you want to accomplish and you want to have happen, experience the sense that you are not alone. That there is a mighty force and power from the divine that is with you all of the time. Ask from your heart for this power that loves you and supports you and has your best interest in mind to become your partner. So whenever you feel alone, scared, unsafe, overwhelmed, tap into this source that is giving you life right now, that sustains all things and has an intelligence that is incomprehensible to our human mind; an intelligence that makes your body function, that makes the cosmos move. And in this mystery of life that encompasses you and everything else, claim this energy and how it works with you in every aspect of your life.

Imagine what it would be like if you actually claimed that power. How strong you would feel. How courageous you would feel. How fearless you would feel. If there are any areas where you may not feel worthy of this, go there and forgive those parts. It is in asking from our own reverence and humility that we can receive assistance from this energy, this power, this source that is our very life. Stay with that for a moment until it fills your heart, breathe it into your whole being. See yourself going from one thing to another, accomplishing tasks, making things happen, interacting with people, finishing your projects, having more abundance in your life, having better relationships, vital health, greater opportunities. You never walk away. Things align and fall into place miraculously when you ask that power, that energy, that God of yours to partner with you. As you ground it in yourself, give thanks for this knowing and let yourself be happy to know that you are never alone. Forgive yourself for anything you may be holding against yourself; for feeling unworthy, undeserving, or that you have to prove yourself to have this happen. You don't. All it takes is your willingness to ask and assume it. Fill yourself with love right now, all throughout your body. Take a deep breath and exhale. When you're ready, open your eyes, wriggle your fingers and toes, shake your shoulders, roll your head left to right, open your arms, extending them up, and exhale, "Ahh." Give yourself a big hug, smiling inside and out. Now, you're ready to move forward with your day, knowing that this mighty power of love is with you.

Allow that energy of love and support to meet you in your need because it knows every need and will meet you there.

48.

BE A MASTER MANIFESTOR

Whether you think you can, or you think you can't—you're right.

—Henry Ford

If you want to manifest something new in your life, such as a fit body, the right partner, a new career, more money, or a new home, you have to start with the belief that what you desire is possible. You must overcome the critical voice that says you can't do or have that.

There are countless living examples of people who have overcome tremendous obstacles to realize their dream, often prevailing over a personal challenge and turning it into a vision to serve humanity. Consider Pakistani student Malala Yousafzai, who was persecuted and even shot for advocating education for women and has since become the youngest ever Noble Prize Laureate. Claire Wineland, another teenager, has lived with incurable cystic fibrosis from birth and wasn't expected to reach her eighteenth birthday. She's now eighteen years old and has not only written a book and appeared on talk shows nationwide but has also created Claire's Place Foundation, a nonprofit dedicated to helping others with cystic fibrosis. And we all remember Erin Brockovich. Not only was she instrumental in a successful legal action against PG&E for leaking chromium into the groundwater in Hinkley,

California, making thousands of people sick, she continues to address other threatening environmental issues. In order to manifest their vision, each of these women has moved out of her comfort zone. Likewise, you have to be willing to become uncomfortable in order to do what you have never done before.

In order to manifest what you want, start by creating a positive intention. Manifesting begins with the knowledge that you are a creator. We are a part of the divine intelligence—the Source, the One, God. As you allow yourself to become more aware of this powerful reality, you can choose to partner with that intelligence, claim it, affirm it, and start to live more consciously in a way that moves you toward your desired outcome.

There are a couple important steps in the art of manifesting. First, come into agreement with all parts of yourself—your mind, heart, spirit, even body—so that all of you can work cooperatively to go after what you want. You can't move forward with one foot stuck in the mud.

Second, imagine what you want. Imagine means "to image in," to bring what you want closer to you. Start by building a repetitive pattern in your mind of pictures, beliefs, and feelings connected to the experience you want to have. For example, if you desire more business clients, envision what it would feel like to have more clients. What does this look like? What is the emotional and mental state you are in when you have more clients? What actions do you need to take to make this image a reality? See it, feel it, visualize it until you become it.

My sister was fifteen years old when she decided that she wanted to study economics at Cambridge—at a time when we were living in a little one-bedroom apartment in Athens. That summer, our mother took my sister to England to visit Cambridge and encouraged her to imagine what it would be like to live there. They interacted with students, ate on campus, and walked around acting as though my sister was already admitted to the school. Intuitively, my mother knew that in order to manifest something, you have to experience it, to bring it as close to you as possible, as if you were holding it in your hand. She was right. She was also right in knowing that vision without the right actions didn't add to manifestation. With a lot of dedication, discipline, and devotion in her studies to prepare for the exams, my sister got into Cambridge.

Each morning, set your intention and the vision that you want for your day. Start your day not on automatic pilot, but with conscious choices of what you want to accomplish. Maybe you simply see yourself in a good mood or connecting with all the right people, or visualize finishing a project that has been nagging you. Perhaps you simply want to be able to handle things in a more centered way. Make the ideal theme of your day as real as possible, and invite your higher self, the "creator" who knows how to manifest, to partner with you the same way that you would ask a friend for help. I've gotten into the habit of writing down the three to four things I want in a day, as well as the longer-term vision of what I want for my life. Then I watch to see how they miraculously start to unfold.

Preparation meets opportunity. I don't believe in such a thing as luck. People whom we call lucky have set a clear intention of what they want. The universe resonates with what you put out, so be cognizant of what you ask for.

If you are trying to manifest something and it isn't happening, be honest with yourself and question your motivation. Is this something that aligns with your purpose and integrity? Or is it something that is ego driven, coming from a need to be recognized in the world? Ultimately the thing that you desire should be connected to your heart. If it brings you joy thinking about it, you will find ways to make it happen.

Make sure you aren't ambivalent about what you want to create. If you are having a challenging time manifesting what you desire, evaluate your beliefs and intentions. For example, let's say you want to manifest your ideal partner, but part of you believes that you are unworthy of love. Then you won't manifest this person. Or if you want to be promoted, but you don't really believe you are capable, then you won't be promoted. Shed some light into the undercurrents of your beliefs that could be blocking you from manifesting what you want. Sit down and have a good conversation with yourself. Get to know what is going on in there. Find a safe place to air out your conflicting intentions.

Once you resolve your issues, you can move forward with enthusiasm. One of my favorite Greek words is *entheos*, which means "within God." Enthusiasm is the wind that energizes your vision. Your enthusiasm spiritualizes the thing you want. Charge your vision with your spirit and devotion, and know that in this state of mind, not only are you paving the way for your vision to be fulfilled, but you are also expanding to attract opportunities to come your way.

Manifesting doesn't happen through pushing, or "powering through." Manifesting isn't the same as ambition. It's being connected to intention. Doubts and insecurities may surface on your way to obtaining your goal, but simply observe them—don't feed them with negative energy and fear. As the Bible says, "As a man thinketh in his heart, he becometh." Our brain doesn't know the difference between a thing happening in our imagination or in reality. Your imagination is a great tool to rehearse the way you want things to be. Start acting as if you already have what you want and then you will start to embody it.

Einstein said, "Imagination is more powerful than knowledge." The women I mentioned earlier have been able to imagine themselves not only rising above extreme challenges, but going beyond their limited self and tapping into a larger vision of what could be. So can you.

Don't be lazy and don't blame the universe when things don't appear to be going your way. Manifesting is as vigorous as if you were training for the Olympics. You might fall and lose yourself a little bit, but pick yourself up and keep going the distance. You are training your mind to be consistent and focused and to stay the course. Nothing must get in the way. Let your vision be aligned with and anchored in your purpose. As you continue to bring it close, trust that the universe will eventually match you and you will know the power of becoming a master manifestor!

SUGGESTIONS FOR THIS WEEK

1. Get completely clear about what you want. See it—"image in"—in detail, like a master craftsman or a painter. Take some quality time to write in your journal, meditate, or just sit down with a good cup of tea and envision what you want.

2. Feel it, in all ways! Write in your journal how you feel emotionally, mentally, and physically when you have exactly what you want. Use all your senses and be as kinesthetic as possible. See it, touch it, feel it as real. Practice living and behaving as though you have already attained your vision. Embody it.

3. Experience it through your actions. Make a plan of specific things you can do to bring your goal into life so that it feels as real as possible even before it happens. Onward, forward, and inward.

ༀ

GUIDED MEDITATION

Find a comfortable position where you can sit relaxed and won't be interrupted for a little while. Allow your mind to become relaxed and soften your heart and emotions. Bring your energy present into your heart and body. As you take a deep breath, relax even deeper.

Observe the rise and fall of your breath. Start to activate your ability to visualize what it is that you would like to have in your life. Pick something that is one of your wishes or dreams. Bring that desire into close proximity.

See the pictures in your mind of what needs to happen to make this desire come true. Experience your fullness and sense these feelings in your belly. Do you feel safe having what you wished for? Do you feel worthy? Can you envision your action steps?

Envision people you know coming to your aid. Open the field of generosity toward yourself. Know that you can receive support and assistance in any area. If your mind says, "I don't know how," allow the part of you that knows to show you how.

Pay attention to your consciousness to see if you are resisting your vision because it might mean you need to make more effort, let go of comfort, or make yourself vulnerable. Whatever it is, allow yourself to be honest to see if this is something you really don't desire.

You don't need to have it all figured out. Simply have an alignment with your intentions. Your higher self will support and assist you if your vision is for your highest good.

Ask yourself if there is something that you need to know

for your desire to materialize. As you build those pictures in your mind, ask if there is a next step. Whatever it is, just listen. As you take your next breath, consciously breathe deeply into your belly, all the way down to your toes, and fill your brain with new wavelengths of pictures, emotions, and thoughts that can transport you to this other reality to experience what you want. Make it so alive in you that it feels like a reality. Take your hands and place your right hand on your belly, and your left on your heart, and with the power of your breath—the power of your life—infuse this vision of yourself with love, enthusiasm, and compassion. Allow yourself to know that it is with your heartfelt leadership that you will move forward with joy in manifesting your vision. You're anchoring this in your body so whenever you have a feeling of not being connected to what you want to manifest, you can return to your heart and belly, because your vision is now anchored there. Connect often with the part of you that carries your vision so it can be activated.

When you are ready, take a deep breath, smile inside and out, exhale, and when you open your eyes, see the world with a new perception of what it will be like to live with what you desire. Wriggle your hands, your feet, stretch your neck, take a sip of water.

Take a moment to remember that you can return to this experience anytime you want.

49

THERE'S ALWAYS A SOLUTION

I can imagine it working out perfectly, I said. I can't, she said, and I said no wonder you're so stressed.

—Brian Andreas

Have you ever misplaced your keys? You frantically look around and, of course, they're in your handbag. Or you can't find your passport or your wallet. When you're about to board the plane, you have a moment of panic—where has your boarding pass gone? You start to feel hot, your mind starts racing . . . and then you find it in your pocket. Everything's fine.

I often experience this anxiety that comes out of nowhere to consume me. You know how it goes. It takes over your body, your brain vibrates with fear. It's irrational; there is no natural disaster, nothing truly awful has occurred. When this happens, I have trained myself to stop, breathe, and have a little chat with myself. I start by asking myself, what is the root of all of this anxiety? Where did it start? What is its origin? And what is it telling me?

The answer that often comes is that I have not been present with myself to what's really going on; I am moving too fast or on autopilot or I have a concern that I haven't made conscious.

And I need to remind myself that there's always a solution. It's something I learned when I was young, from my mother. When I return to that trust, it brings me a wave of calm.

My mother had an amazing ability to see the solutions to situations that could have been paralyzing. One Saturday evening when I was a teenager, my mom was taking my sister and me to the theater. No sooner had we closed the door to the apartment than my mother asked my sister, "Do you have my handbag?" My sister said, "No, I thought you had it." We all realized we had locked my mother's handbag inside the apartment along with the money, keys, and tickets. The normal reaction would be to get upset and say, "We can't go to dinner or to the theater and now we have to get a locksmith. Our evening is ruined." But that was not my mother. Not missing a beat, she went straight to the resident manager and asked her to borrow some money for the evening. We got into a taxi. My sister and I kept asking, "How do we get into the theater? How do we get into the apartment?" But wisely, confidently, my mother said, "Don't worry, we will find a way."

We arrived at the theater and she told the box office manager exactly what had happened. She knew the row and seat numbers. Out of the kindness of his heart, the manager checked to see if there were any open seats. Indeed, our seats were open, and we went in and enjoyed the wonderful play! She had borrowed enough money for dinner and a taxi home.

On our ride home, we asked, "Mommy, how are we going to get back into our apartment?" Well, we were lucky that we lived across from the fire department. When we arrived home, Mom went over there and asked for help. The firefighters put up a ladder to the third floor, opened our window, got into the apartment, and opened the door for us. My sister and I were amazed by the night, and seeing our amazement, she said in her wise way, "Remember, there is always a solution and never a need to panic." To thank the firemen, my mom sent over cookies—a Greek tradition.

Years later, all grown up, I was leaving Las Vegas after conducting a workshop and returning to L.A., where I had to give a speech. When I arrived at the airport, I found out that my flight had been canceled. The flight after mine was booked solid, and the next available flight would get me to L.A. after my speech was scheduled. Remembering my mom's counsel that there is always a solution, I approached the counter, where many people were venting their frustration to the attendant. I went to the side, waited for a moment when the attendant was not completely preoccupied, and handed him my book, *Conversations with the Goddesses.* I said, "Hi, my name is Agapi and I'm the author of this book, and I would like to give you a copy in exchange for getting me on the next flight. I'm on a book tour and I have a speech to get to and can't miss it." I shook his hand and he looked at me with openness and said, "Let me take a look. Stay here."

A few minutes later, he said to me, "How would you like to get on the flight before the one that was canceled? It leaves in fifteen minutes. I got you a seat. Your luggage won't make it but you will!"

Fifteen minutes later I was on a flight to L.A. I arrived without my perfect book tour outfit, but earlier than my original flight would have gotten me there. How did that happen? Who made it happen? I don't know exactly, but I do know it comes from a place of calm. When you free your mind of panic, fear, frustration, you'll see solutions, find ways, know which turn to take and which words to say. You'll hear the whisper of your creative mind. Not only that, you'll meet deadlines, arrive on time, and somehow take the route where there is no traffic. This is called being in alignment with the universal flow. It happens when you allow for space and openness, for the universe to present itself in a new way.

Know that there's always a solution; amazing things will happen. Everything will fall into place, and that's what I call grace.

GUIDED MEDITATION

Find a comfortable position. Turn off your devices. Take a deep breath. As you exhale, exhale the tensions, the worries, the concerns of your day. Bring your heart present and start to attune to your breath, the rising and falling of your breath, bring your awareness to an issue, or a problem you are experiencing. It could be related to health, a relationship, work, finances, real estate, anything that comes present. Take a deep breath and bring this issue present in your consciousness. Breathe into it grace, love, compassion, and bring it to the light. Start to let it go right now. Just exhale and as you exhale, let it go.

Rise inside yourself to a place where you feel more detached. You begin to feel more centered, more supported. Tell yourself: it's okay that this issue, this problem exists in my life. It's okay. I don't have to fight it. I don't have to solve it. I don't have to manipulate it. I don't have to do anything about it. I am here, I am alive, and I am breathing. So, I am fine. Your mind might want to bring it back, saying, "You can't be calm, you need to worry. What are you going to do about this?" and it's up to you to address your mind and say, "Relax, I got this." As you keep attuning to your breath, allow yourself the space, the knowledge, the inner wisdom to know that the solution will appear. The answer of what you need to do will show up. Give yourself permission, right now, to know that the solution will appear in perfect timing. Smile inside and outside, and affirm: "I am bigger than this. I know help is coming. Solutions are coming. I am willing to let go." Listen to your wisdom, to your guidance, to your intuition. Take as much time as you need to listen. As you exhale, center in your heart, experience the calmness that is present, knowing that all is well and solutions are coming to you.

Breathe in this calmness to the core of your being, to your belly, where a lot of feelings reside, and cover them with a canopy of peace, love, and profound stillness. Breathe it in all the way to the bottom of your feet, up and down your spine, fill your brain with this peace, from the top of your head to the bottom of your feet and all around you, you are protected and filled with calmness and a loving presence. As you anchor this feeling, inside and out, take a deep breath, fill your lungs with air, and gently, slowly exhale, wriggle your toes, your hands, stretch your neck left and right, gently shake your shoulders, take a deep breath and exhale, and as you exhale open your eyes and sigh . . . "Ahh." Come back into the room and smile, inside and out.

You may want to drink some water to ground yourself. You also may want to take your journal and jot down anything that you've heard, saw, or felt, or any intuitions or wisdoms that showed up. Be willing to know that you know what to do or not to do, and that you have access to all the tools and keys for your life.

50.

REVERENCE, GRATITUDE, AND OMG

Gratitude bestows reverence, allowing us to encounter everyday epiphanies, those transcendent moments of awe that change forever how we experience life and the world.

—John Milton

Unless you're an actor on *The Big Bang Theory* or a scientist working on the Hubble telescope, you probably tend not to think about the vastness of the universe on a daily basis. So I'd like to blow your mind with some facts about the universe. A galaxy is a vast grouping of stars, and there are 200 billion galaxies in the universe. There are approximately 1,000,000,000,000,000, 000,000,000 (that's twenty-four zeroes) planets in the universe and something like 100 billion trillion stars. There are more stars than grains of sand on the beach. We are living in an awe-inspiring and unimaginably large universe.

Contemplating the immensity of our cosmos can make you feel very small and insignificant. However, think about this: You have 37.2 trillion cells in your body. There's vastness outside you and vastness inside you. You are connected to this mystery and miracle. You are a microcosm of the universe, and every aspect of your life benefits from the universe's provision.

I don't often tune into the cosmos. I leave that to the scientists. However, when I do think about these things, it fills me with an extraordinary feeling of reverence, gratitude, and OMG. It shifts me from taking things for granted to the profound awareness that I get to enjoy and participate in this miraculous experience of life. That I didn't create any of this. So I might as well marvel at the wonder and be humbled by it.

We all get caught in complaining about how things are not going our way and should be different, which takes us away from our gratitude. This pulls us into entitlement, blaming, and demanding, shutting off the current that connects us to the source of creation. Once I was traveling to Montana to speak at a big hospital. Everything went wrong; my flight was canceled, so I had to go home and come back to the airport for the morning flight. The next day, when heading home after my talk, I had a connecting flight in Salt Lake City that was delayed until the morning. I was going to be stuck in the airport all night, so I started complaining internally, thinking, "I can't believe this is happening again. This has been such a hard trip. What am I going to do now?" I was spiraling. Suddenly, I heard a little voice inside me say, "Start thanking everything."

I realized it was a command from my spirit. I complied, saying, "Okay, I'm going to start thanking everything. Let's start with the fact that my plane landed here in Salt Lake City safely. Thank you that my phone still has a charge and I can call people. Thank you for all the people I touched in Montana. Thank you that my carry-on is still with me. Thank you that I have a chair to sit in and can think of what to do next. Thank you that I'm not in a wheelchair or on crutches."

As I continued to be thankful, suddenly the phone rang. It was a friend of mine asking me where I was. I said to him, "I'm in Salt Lake City stuck in the airport." He said, "That's funny because I'm arriving in Salt Lake City in three hours. Why don't you go and stay in my hotel suite. I'll happily sleep on the couch and bring you to the airport in the morning." Wow! Three minutes of gratitude turned everything around.

After this experience, I decided to regularly practice thankfulness. On my way back to New York, I gave thanks for the pilots, the flight attendants, the snacks they serve, the terrible coffee—at least it was hot. I was just thanking everything and everyone. What a wonderful way to go through life. I found myself smiling as if I had been handed a golden key. Now, whenever I'm worried, anxious, or complaining, I remind myself of how this precious key can unlock my gratitude. Sometimes I write down what I'm thankful for. However you do it, every time you say "thank you," you're exercising and strengthening your gratitude muscle.

There have been numerous studies done that show that gratitude increases self-esteem, improves physical, mental and psychological health, enhances empathy, reduces aggression, and helps with better sleep. In short, gratitude is the fastest way to happiness. As my mother used to say, "If you are unhappy, be grateful. Because you can't be grateful and unhappy at the same time." Here's what I'm grateful for right now: my breath, babies, children running around, extra virgin olive oil, contact lenses, running water, soap, TV, safe streets, bathtubs, trees, loved ones, strangers who become friends, cappuccinos, elevators, Facebook, scissors, anesthesia, meditation, Pharrell's song "Happy," Gibran, Mozart, Spanx, honey, lemon trees, butterflies, the Aegean Sea and on and on. . . . Be thankful for the obstacles, tests, and challenges. When people around you push your buttons and you start to react, find the gratitude underneath the irritation. As Dr. Robert Emmons said, "To say we feel grateful is not to say that everything in our lives is necessarily great. It just means we are aware of our blessings."

Sometimes you might say your thank-yous and not really feel it 100 percent, but if you make a habit of this practice, you will eventually be flooded by heartfelt gratitude. Think of all the people who have lived before you who have contributed to your life. Think how amazing it is to live in freedom, creativity, abundance, ingenuity, and enjoyment. Living in gratitude is the transformative ingredient to making your life magical.

SUGGESTIONS FOR THIS WEEK

1. Pick a day and decide to spend the whole day running "thank you" as a mantra in your heart and mind. Start to notice all of the things you take for granted; thank yourself, thank others, give thanks for all the little things around you, the opportunities that have come your way, all you've been gifted with, the relationships in your life. By the end of the day, write down in your journal how shifting to gratitude changed the flow of your energy and day.

2. When you find yourself complaining, shift into gratitude about the little things in your life, and be thankful for all the things that you don't want and you don't have.

3. Take an object: a book, sweater, glass, pen, the house, and think about how many people it took to create, design, and execute this object. For a book: start with the trees and the elaborate ingenuity it takes to produce paper, the content, the

editing, the printing press, the design of the cover, the publishing house, the writer, the bookstore, the distribution service to get it to you. Do this practice with the things around
you to develop an appreciation for the collaborative effort that
goes into creating one thing. Learn about the process by which
something is made. Google "How is paper made?" and you'll
never waste another sheet again!

4. Pick five people in your life and write them a "thank-you" letter. Acknowledge them and tell them how much you appreciate them. Words matter. This will surprise and delight them.
Make this a sacred, heartfelt experience that can move you
into deep gratitude.

GUIDED MEDITATION

Find a comfortable place where you won't be interrupted
for a little while. Center yourself in yourself. Relax your
body and your emotions. Let go of any tension and any
concerns of the day. Envision a beautiful warm white light.
Ask that this light fill you, surround you, and protect you,
bringing a sense of deep calmness, and safety. Open up
your creative imagination and start to imagine the vastness
of the universe. There you are sitting in the space where
you are, but let your mind expand into the vast universe
that surrounds us. Two hundred billion galaxies. Billions and
trillions of planets. A hundred billion trillion stars. And this
little planet Earth revolving around the powerful energy of
the sun. Wow. Take a moment to be in awe of the vastness
of it all, and that it is in constant motion. Unimaginable and

awe-inspiring. The only response to this inexplicable mystery of the universe is reverence. A deep sense of reverence. And a profound, heartfelt thank-you. As you take your next breath, consider this: where does your breath come from? Your breath of life without which you cannot exist. There is no answer. None of us know. It is freely given. And the only response is, Thank You.

As you take your next breath, breathe in this immense gratitude for the gift of your life. As you exhale, let your gratefulness overflow. Let your heart soften, take in the awe, the wonder of it all. Take your two hands and clasp them together. Your fingers, aren't they amazing, these fingers? They move, they have bones and skin and nails. Feel your hands and be in awe of your hands. Your feet, your knees that bend, your neck that turns left and right, your amazing shoulders, your elbows. What a miracle. Your eyes, that they can see, they see colors. They open and they close. Your vocal cords, they make sounds. Your mouth that forms words that communicate thoughts. Your ears, that hear millions of different sounds. What a miracle we are. The only response is, Thank You.

Start to see and feel how much you have to be grateful for, and go down the list of all the extraordinary things around your life that you might be taking for granted. The chair you are sitting on right now. How many people it took to make the chair. How did it get to your place? Imagine. Just that simple chair. The design, the manufacturing, the hands that made it, the people who delivered it to your place. And the only response is, Thank You.

Think of the water you drink in a glass. Clean water, how

did it get there? Where did it come from? How many people did it take to get that water to you? There are millions and millions of people who don't have access to clean water. And yet for us it is a given. The only response is, Thank You. Thank you.

Start to make an endless list in your life about all the little things to the big things, and of course to all the people around you. Your relationships. Even if there are hard times, even if there is conflict, isn't it wonderful that you are surrounded by so many people, each one of them is so unique. Look at their faces and see the humanity under every face. Let your heart be filled with this extraordinary gift of humanity. Send waves of light and love and gratitude about all the humans you meet every day. Your loved ones, strangers, people at the supermarket; be in reverence of it all. Let your light shine on every aspect of your life. On every strand of your hair. Issue a deep prayer inside that as you walk in your daily life, you will remember not to take anything for granted, but to live in this immense gratitude and reverence and awe, and that you will be blessed to know the mystery of life in you and all around you. Ask that this mystery of who you are and this miraculous universe you are part of be revealed to you. Bow to this universal energy that makes all things come to light, and you get to partake. And in this stillness, and in this place of deep surrender, listen to your higher wisdom, which is always there. Pause throughout the day to listen, to connect, and to cultivate this gift of gratitude.

As you fill yourself with this good joyful feeling, gently open your eyes and become present in the room. Maybe now you notice things you've never noticed before. Little details around you. Remembering how many people's efforts and journeys it took to make everything around you possible. Walk in your day with your heart resonating thank you. Thank you. Silently do your day as a thank-you. Drink some water to ground yourself. Wriggle your beautiful fingers, and tell them thank you. Wriggle your toes and feet, and say thank you. Turn your neck left and right, and stand, stretch and say thank you. Open your arms and embrace yourself and say thank you. And if you would like, pick up your pen and say thank you. And your beautiful journal, and write your thank-you list for the day, or anything else that has been revealed to you. When you go out into the world, take a moment and look at the sky. We so rarely look at the sky. Let yourself wonder and be in awe.

51

THE VIEW FROM THE YEAR 3005

We are not human beings having a spiritual experience. We are spiritual beings having a human experience.

—Pierre Teilhard de Chardin

Do you ever feel like time is flying by? Like today it's winter and before you know it, it's summer, and you think, "Where has the time gone?" I am so often hit by the fleeting nature of time, how quickly our precious life flies by and the fact that all of "this" will end. This inexplicable truth gives me perspective.

We have no control over how or when our life will end. But we know that we will all die. The ancient Romans understood not just that we are not immortal, but that it's important to remember our mortality, and they carved MM, for *memento mori*—"Remember death"—on statues and trees. They put every victory and every defeat into its proper perspective. Did you ever have a teacher ask, "How do you feel about death? What is your perspective on life? What do you think the purpose of your life is? How do you want to live your life?" I never had a teacher who asked me these fundamental questions until I met my spiritual teacher. The subject is never discussed in our schools and colleges, so we live as though our life as we know it will never change and we are immortal. We are always mortified and shocked when someone dies suddenly, and that's because we're not educated about the topic of death or taught to live with the reality that we will all die. Instead, we avoid it, hide from it, and ignore it. Imagine the profound effect it could have on our daily choices and decisions, as well as our values, if we lived with this awareness every day. We might be able to get back to the essentials of life and what truly matters to us!

Dealing with our mortality instead of running from it can be very liberating. It removes some of the tension from the daily tasks that we make so overly important. I learned this when I was going through a very challenging time. I had left L.A. to be with a man I thought was "the one," but within six months the relationship disintegrated and I realized that he wasn't for me. There I was—on my own, in my early forties, without my family, starting life over again. I began to doubt and pressure myself with questions like "Why am I not married?" "Why am I not getting it together?" I felt extremely vulnerable and very alone. I thought, "That's it. I'll never find anybody."

One day, I hit such a low point that I couldn't even reach out to friends. In that crashing moment, I closed the curtains, lit a candle, lay on my couch, and asked for help from the very deepest part of me. In full surrender, I said, "Please help me. I don't know what to do." I had hit rock bottom. I didn't know where else to turn. I let myself sink into the couch, just let go, and my tears began to flow.

Within the quietness around me, without even realizing it, I had made a space for the inner light of my soul to enter. I slowly began to feel warmth, comfort, love, and connection. The inner curtain was lifting and my soul was answering my plea. I saw a house very high up in the mountains, and an amazing vista with a calm and beautiful lake. Everything was crystal clear. I heard my soul whisper, "It is the year 3005 and life on earth has evolved. The people you knew have traveled into other realities. You have had many journeys since your last time on earth." In an instant, time had expanded. My feelings of being alone, hurt, and disconnected started to dissolve in the comfort of this bigger reality. I felt free of fear. I was taken into the future without ever leaving my apartment in New York City. I started to remember my true connection to my purpose in life: to know, love, and connect with myself.

During this experience, the pain, disappointment, and hopelessness released—like space opening around my heart. As this happened, I felt an even greater sense of relief, euphoria, and comfort. This was the first time I experienced the truth that we really do live forever. That we do not die. We are eternal, just a breath away from knowing our soul.

When I returned from this experience, I felt elated and grounded at the same time. Although my mind grappled to find the memory of the pain and loneliness I had been feeling, it wasn't there. For me, this was a moment of grace, where time and reality had expanded, and I understood how timeless we all are and how transitory our experience of being on the earth is. I felt like my very brain cells were shifting, and was very grateful that my spirit had given me such a vivid and memorable experience that I could recall any time I wanted.

This extraordinary experience seeped into the ordinariness of my everyday life. I got up from the couch, went into the kitchen, and started to do the dishes. I wrote in my journal, beginning with the phrase, "It was the year 3005 . . ." My life went on. I published my first book. Friends and family went through ups and downs. My parents, still living at the time, eventually encountered illness. I had a hard time seeing them deteriorate and die, and the year after they died was extremely difficult. But the "Year 3005" experience is with me, embedded in my heart, reminding me of a bigger reality and a perspective that helps me relinquish that sense of separateness. As we dissolve the separateness, we start to feel connected to something larger than ourselves, and this makes us trust that we are guided, protected, and on the right path. This is very liberating, and gives us a glimpse into just how creative we can be, and how much more fun we can have with this precious life of ours. *There is no light at the end of the tunnel. We are the light in the tunnel and as we go through the darkness, our light guides us.*

I am sharing this experience with you so it may trigger your own ability to go beyond the time and space of where you are now, into the bigger reality of timelessness. This is not something that is bestowed only upon mystics, scientists, or people who study cosmic consciousness. This ability is a reality that is available to anyone who seeks it. All you have to do is pause and tap into the bigger reality within you, open yourself, and choose to go there in your creative imagination. And see what happens! Your heart can open wide enough for your perception to expand and shift, gracefully ushering you into a new perspective. This knowledge and awareness can leave you feeling more relaxed, compassionate, more in awe of the mystery of your life, and yet feeling responsible for what you need to handle in this life. You can become anchored in a sense of the greater whole that you are a part of because you are less afraid.

In that moment on my couch I surrendered and asked for help. It is in the asking that our soul will hear the call and meet us.

Maybe we have to ask a few times until that part of us wakes up, but *it won't let us down.* The spirit will hear our sincerity and rise to greet us, revealing the truth in our time of need.

The year 3005 will come and you won't be the person you know today. This is just a fact. I hope it fills you with awe, appreciation, fearlessness, and the freedom to enjoy your life from a new perspective.

GUIDED MEDITATION

Find a comfortable position in a quiet space. You could even lie on a couch or on your bed, wherever you won't be interrupted for a little while, and as you attune yourself to your breath, become present in your heart. Ask for a beautiful warm light to fill you, surround you, and protect you. Ask for the presence of your soul. Make space inside of you to receive the presence of your soul. Let go of the tensions of your day, any worries. This is a moment for you to be in your presence. To let your presence fill you. Ask for the presence of your creative imagination.

Imagine that there is a veil separating this reality from an eternal reality where your soul has lived, and is living. The eternal reality is expansive, it's big, it's way larger than the way you experience yourself in this physical world. Lift your eyes and your consciousness to the top of your head. Imagine that you're being guided to lift this veil between the two realities. As it lifts, imagine what it would be like in the year 3005. That's almost one thousand years away from now, when you won't be here; those you know won't be here; and the earth will be ever so different.

Imagine yourself, in your soul's presence, moving rapidly through time and space, where year after year, things are unfolding, and ask yourself, "Who am I then? This person that I so identify with . . . This self I call myself won't be the same in one thousand years. Who will I be? Who am I if I'm not this self right now?" See yourself living on from now, in the essence and presence of who you are, in the spirit of who you are, that knows and loves you. This spirit will live on. Allow this spirit to be present with you right now, ever so calm and quiet, the spirit is showing you another dimension. You might not see anything, but intuitively, you might experience your aliveness beyond this world. Experience this reality expanding—an awareness that is large, warm, that is like an ocean, that is compassionate—and you are free. You see a path in front of you, lit up with so much light, and you start to experience the beauty of who you are—the beauty of your soul. It permeates you and radiates from inside out.

Take a deep breath and let this soul allow you to go to new places you may not have seen before. Ask in your heart if there's anything you want to know. Who you really are. The reality of a vaster truth. Ask your soul, "Is there anything you want to show me?" Allow your soul to reveal to you anything that it wants to reveal. No effort. No pushing. Just allowing. It might be an intuition, a sound, a sigh, a symbol. Your soul might want to show you something. If there's nothing, just be in its presence, quiet, compassionate, and joyful. Stay there for a few moments. Bask in the light. Just bask in it. Take deep breaths, letting it come more fully into your life, right now, right here.

When you're ready, open your eyes, wriggle your fingers

and toes, but stay in your presence. You can stretch your neck, left and right. Make a sound to come fully present. Open your arms and bring more of that energy into your body. Say, "Ahh." Take a deep breath again, take a sip of water to ground yourself. Take your journal and write down any insights about the journey you just took.

52

THIS IS
YOUR PRECIOUS
LIFE

Feast on the food you love.
Make your home a sanctuary.
Bring your heart to your workplace.
Love the clothes you're wearing.
Create relationships where you feel cherished.
Bake cookies for people.
Don't wait for special occasions to celebrate.
Do things that remind you of the beauty of life, often.

Let not a day pass without thinking of how precious life is, and how precious the lives of those around you are. We all know that life can be taken suddenly, in an instant. Make each day count. Express your love for your family and friends. Forgive yourself and forgive others. Don't make your precious life harder than it has to be. Experience your day with so much love, gratitude, and compassion that it becomes precious.

Keep your heart open and nourished. Acknowledge people for who they are, what they give. Appreciate them warmly. Be a generous giver. Open doors for people whenever you can. Romance yourself. Wiggle your hips and rejoice in the ability to move. Shake your shoulders when they start to bear the burden of the world. Laugh a lot. When you are sad, cry. Then come back to the gift of your precious life. Speak your truth and stand by it. No matter what you're going through, no matter what challenges you may be facing, no matter your fears and doubts, your insecurities or sense of lack, wake up every morning and go to sleep every night saying, "This is my precious life. This life was given to me. In this precious life I can choose for myself to live in whatever way I want to live. I don't need to prove my worth to anyone. I choose to do things that make me happy, that uplift me, that mean something to me. This life was given to me to live, to enjoy, to learn, to love, to share, to receive, and to give."

This is your precious life and you have every right to live it in the way that works for you. Not looking left and right for other people to tell you what to do. Looking into yourself, to the place where you know the answers.

This is your precious life. Live it. Sing your song. Give it your deepest gratitude. Celebrate your fullness.

GUIDED MEDITATION

Find a comfortable position and take a few moments to attune yourself to the presence of your own breath.

So often we go about our daily life demanding of ourselves that we do better, rushing from one thing to another, and forgetting to take in the amazing gift of what our life is all about. Right now, let's take a moment and open up to experience this miracle of life that is so freely given to us. Nothing to do, no things to accomplish, just a sense of being in awe of the breath of your life, the ability to move, to see, to speak, to form words that can evoke our feelings. To hear the sounds and to marvel at everything you see, and everything that forms this amazing world of ours. Allow yourself to come to the present with yourself. How did you get to be the way you are? That no matter what's happening or not happening, you are alive. You are alive. You can shout, "I am alive!" Isn't it wonderful to be alive? What if you were to let go of all your conditions requiring that things should be different and look at the people around you just the way they are: the people you love, who love you, and say what a privilege it is to be alive. To touch. To love. To hold close the ones you love. To tell them how much you love them. To tell yourself how much you love you. What a privilege to open up your heart and take all of your gifts, to claim that this is your precious life. So short. It goes so fast day after day, so savor it. Make this promise to yourself: you will find joy in the simplest, most ordinary things like looking at a flower, looking at the clouds, having clean water to drink, looking in the mirror and saying, "Good morning, this is my precious life and today is going to be wonderful." Imagine what life would be like if you lived with that principle in mind, to never take anything for granted. Why not start right now?

Take a deep breath, say "thank you" to yourself, to the life that breathes you, to everything and everyone around you, fill your heart with this gratitude and when you're ready, you can open your eyes. Smile a big smile and hug yourself, saying, "This is my precious life. I am going to enjoy every minute of it."

Drink some water so you can ground yourself; be grateful for this water and go about rejoicing in your precious life.

ACKNOWLEDGMENTS

Thank you to the countless people I met while I was on the road for *Unbinding the Heart* who shared with me their struggles and their stories, and what they wanted more of in their lives. They gave me the inspiration for this book.

To my wonderful agent, Bill Gladstone, who met the idea with his enthusiasm and unwavering positive energy. To Diana Baroni, editorial director of Harmony Books, who saw the vision of what this book could be. To my wonderful editor, Donna Loffredo, who brought her brilliant ideas to this book and was such a joy to collaborate with. I met Charity Golden at a women's conference and immediately felt her spirit of service and wonderful disposition. She started working with me, listened with devotion, and brought her insightful feedback in the process of constructing the book. I'm grateful to her for her commitment to this work. To my wonderful tribe of friends who read parts of the manuscript and brought their insight: Melba Alhonte, Faith Bethlard, Cinzia Brandi, Claudia Chan, Beth Grossman, Michael Hays, Joey Hubbard, Paul Kaye, Elaine Lipworth, Alexi Panos, Shelly Reid, Danny Shea, Jan Shepherd, and Joan Witkowski. To Patty

Gift, for her early thoughts and support. And to Parthenia Hicks and Kee Kee Buckley, who worked with me to bring their expert edits to some of the chapters.

To my sister, Arianna, for her love and support, and for always reminding me to sleep so I can have more energy to create. And to my nieces, Isabella and Christina, who help me tap into my joy on a daily basis and put everything in perspective.

ABOUT THE AUTHOR

AGAPI STASSINOPOULOS is a bestselling author and speaker who inspires audiences around the world. In her most recent book, *Unbinding the Heart: A Dose of Greek Wisdom, Generosity, and Unconditional Love*, she shares wisdom from her life's adventures and experiences. Agapi was trained in London at the Royal Academy of Dramatic Art and then moved on to receive her master's degree in psychology from the University of Santa Monica. Her previous books on the Greek archetypes, *Gods and Goddesses in Love* and *Conversations with the Goddesses*, were turned into PBS specials. She is currently conducting workshops for Thrive Global, a company founded by her sister, Arianna Huffington, to help change the way we live and work. Agapi speaks worldwide empowering people to live the lives they want. She divides her time between New York and Los Angeles and was born and raised in Athens, Greece.

FIND HER online at WakeUptotheJoyofYou.com.

Praise for
Wake Up to the Joy of You

"Open this book at any chapter and you will tap into your calm and joy, no matter what challenges you may be facing."
—Elizabeth Gilbert, author of *Eat, Pray, Love* and *Big Magic*

"Filled with spiritual insights and practical wisdom, Agapi has designed a guide for everyone to navigate the road back to your joy and to your connection with your bigger self. This book is a most valuable companion."
—Deepak Chopra, author of *Super Genes*

"Agapi Stassinopoulos vibrates with life in a way that is contagious. In *Wake Up to the Joy of You*, she offers insights and vitality that serve as vitamins for the heart."
—Mark Nepo, author of *Inside the Miracle* and *The One Life We're Given*

"Agapi's book is like entering a comfort zone for the soul. It is a book filled with portable grace that comes through each meditation."
—Caroline Myss, author of *Anatomy of the Spirit*

"Allow the miracle of meditation and focus to uplevel your joy and your life. Let this marvelous book be your guide."
—Christiane Northrup, M.D., ob/gyn physician and author of the *New York Times* bestsellers *Goddesses Never Age: The Secret Prescription for Radiance, Vitality, and Wellbeing; Women's Bodies, Women's Wisdom;* and *The Wisdom of Menopause*

"*Wake Up to the Joy of You* is full of practical wisdom about living a life of gratitude, generosity, and grace. I felt like I was in a personal conversation with Agapi—which is a real treat."

—Adam Grant, Wharton professor and *New York Times* bestselling author of *Originals* and *Give and Take*

"Ever since I can remember, my sister, Agapi, lit up every room she was in and brought her joy to everyone who crossed her path. In this book she shares her heartfelt wisdom and shows how we are the creators of our lives and the source of our own happiness."

—Arianna Huffington, cofounder of the *Huffington Post* and author of *Thrive* and *The Sleep Revolution*

"Agapi is on a mission to help you find the calm in the chaos that we are all facing today. In this book, Agapi takes you on a journey of mind, body, and spirit to reconnect, heal, and create the change you desire. As you read, you'll be guided by Agapi's loving energy as she shows you how to use tools like meditation, which I strongly believe in and use daily in my own Urban Zen Integrative therapy program."

—Donna Karan

"Wow. This isn't just a book, it's a resource for living your best life. With Agapi's wisdom, joy, and exuberance for life jumping off every page, she'll lead you to how you can create peace, harmony, and balance in every aspect of your life."

—Nick Ortner, *New York Times* bestselling author of *The Tapping Solution*